THE PERSIAN GULF AND PACIFIC ASIA

POWER AND POLITICS IN THE GULF

Christopher Davidson and Dirk Vanderwalle (editors)

After decades of sitting on the sidelines of the international system, the energy-exporting traditional monarchies of the Arab Gulf (Saudi Arabia, the United Arab Emirates, Kuwait, Bahrain, Qatar and Oman) are gradually transforming themselves into regional, and potentially global, economic powerhouses. This series aims to examine this trend while also bringing a consistent focus to the much wider range of other social, political, and economic issues currently facing Arab Gulf societies. Quality research monographs, country case studies, and comprehensive edited volumes have been carefully selected by the series editors in an effort to assemble the most rigorous collection of work on the region.

CHRISTOPHER DAVIDSON

The Persian Gulf and Pacific Asia

From Indifference to Interdependence

HURST & COMPANY, LONDON

First published in the United Kingdom in 2010 by
C. Hurst & Co. (Publishers) Ltd.,
41 Great Russell Street, London, WC1B 3PL
© Christopher Davidson, 2010
All rights reserved.
Printed in India by Imprint Digital

A Cataloguing-in-Publication data record for this book is
available from the British Library.

ISBN: 978-1-84904-099-0

This book is printed using paper from registered sustainable
and managed sources.

www.hurstpub.co.uk

CONTENTS

ACKNOWLEDGEMENTS

Over the course of researching and writing this book, several institutions have been enormously helpful. I would particularly like to thank the Centre for the Study of Global Governance at the London School of Economics and the Kuwait Foundation for the Advancement of Sciences for supporting the publication of a pilot version of this work. My thanks go also to the Graduate School of Asian and African Area Studies at Kyoto University for hosting my research activities in Japan in 2009, and the Tokyo University of Foreign Studies and the Japanese Ministry for Foreign Affairs for extending their full cooperation. But more important than any institutions have been the people who have supported and encouraged me with this project. Dr. Kristian Coates-Ulrichsen for the coordination of peer reviews in addition to logistical assistance and the final layer of constructive criticism. Professor Yashushi Kosugi and Mr. Koji Horinuki for their help in Kyoto. Miss Namie Tsujigami for her help and hospitality in Kobe. Mr. Koji Muto for his help in Tokyo, in particular with the Japanese Ministry for Foreign Affairs. Miss Maja Vodopivec for all her help and wonderful hospitality in Tokyo and all across Japan. Dr. Gordon Cheung, Dr. Yukiko Miyagi, and Professor Anoushivaran Ehteshami in Durham for their advice. Miss Mari Luomi and Mr. David Roberts for their assistance with research. And most importantly, Mr. Michael Dwyer, my truly indefatigable editor at C. Hurst & Co. who somehow manages to keep up with me.

ABBREVIATIONS

ADCO	Abu Dhabi Company for Onshore Oil Operations
ADGAS	Abu Dhabi Gas Liquefaction
ADIA	Abu Dhabi Investment Authority
ADNOC	Abu Dhabi National Oil Company
ADTA	Abu Dhabi Tourism Authority
ALBA	Aluminium Bahrain
AMD	Advanced Micro Devices
ASEAN	Association of Southeast Asian Nations
ATIC	Advanced Technology Investment Company
CCTV-Arabic	China Central TV in Arabic
CEO	chief executive officer
CEPSA	Compañia Española de Petroleos
CNOOC	China National Offshore Oil Corporation
CNPC	China National Petroleum Corporation
CRCC	China Railway Construction Company
DIC	Dubai International Capital
DIFC	Dubai International Finance Centre
DLF	Dhofar Liberation Front
DMCC	Dubai Multi Commodities Centre
DPJ	Democratic Party of Japan
DUBAL	Dubai Aluminium
EDF	Électricité de France
EIA	Energy Information Administration
ENEC	Emirates Nuclear Energy Corporation
FDI	foreign direct investment
FREP	Fujian Refining and Petrochemical Company
FTA	free trade agreement

ABBREVIATIONS

GASCO	Abu Dhabi Gas Industries
GCC	Gulf Cooperation Council
GDF-Suez	Gaz de France-Suez
GDP	gross domestic product
IEA	International Energy Agency
IPIC	International Petroleum Investment Company
JBIC	Japan Bank for International Cooperation
JCCI	Jeddah Chamber of Commerce and Industry
JCCME	Japan Cooperation Centre for the Middle East
JETRO	Japanese External Trade Organization
JODCO	Japanese Oil Development Company
JSF	Joint Strike Fighter
KAIST	Korea Advanced Institute of Science and Technology
KCIC	Kuwait-China Investment Company
KEPCO	Korea Electric Power Corporation
KFAED	Kuwait Fund for Arab Economic Development
KIA	Kuwait Investment Authority
KISR	Kuwait Institute for Scientific Research
KKH	Karakoram Highway
KPC	Kuwait Petroleum Company
KSIA	South Korea Semiconductor Industry Association
KUSTAR	Khalifa University of Science, Technology, and Research
MHI	Mitsubishi Heavy Industries
NBAD	National Bank of Abu Dhabi
NOC	Nippon Oil Corporation
NSCSA	National Shipping Company of Saudi Arabia
ODA	official development assistance
OECD	Organization for Economic Cooperation and Development
OPEC	Organization of Petroleum Exporting Countries
QIA	Qatari Investment Authority
SABIC	Saudi Arabian Basic Industries
SACF	Sino Arab Chemical Fertilizer Company
SBI	Softbank Investment Corporation Holdings
TEDA	Tianjin Economic and Technological Development Area Company
TEPCO	Tokyo Electricity Power Company
UAE	United Arab Emirates

ABBREVIATIONS

UN	United Nations
US	United States
USSR	Union of Soviet Socialist Republics

LIST OF FIGURES

TABLES

CHARTS

INTRODUCTION

A plethora of economic, diplomatic, cultural, and other highly pragmatic link-ages are finally making the long-predicted 'Asianisation' of Asia a reality.[1] As this book will demonstrate, the powerful and multidimensional connections that are being forged by the very eastern and western extremities of the continent are poised to become a central pillar of this process. Given time, this will finally lead to the emergence of meaningful bilateral ties between non-Western poles of the international system,[2] involving states that up until recently had been considered as peripheral to the global economy[3] and dependent on the advanced capitalist countries for their trade and investment.[4] Most notably, an important new relationship is developing between the six monarchies of the Persian Gulf—Saudi Arabia,[5] the United Arab Emirates (UAE),[6] Kuwait,[7] Qatar,[8] Bahrain,[9] and Oman[10]—and the three most advanced economies of Pacific Asia—Japan, China, and South Korea. With little shared modern economic history, with enormous political and socio-economic disparities, and separated by great geographical distances, the rapidly tightening economic interdependence between the two regions is a recent phenomenon that deserves considerable attention. What began as a simple, late twentieth century marriage of convenience based on hydrocarbon imports and exports has now evolved into a comprehensive, long-term mutual commitment that will not only continue to capitalize on the Persian Gulf's rich energy resources and Pacific Asia's massive energy needs, but will also seek to develop strong non-hydrocarbon bilateral trade, will facilitate sizeable sovereign wealth investments in both directions, and will provide lucrative opportunities for experienced Pacific Asian construction companies, their technologies, and—in China's case—its vast labour force.

Although this increasingly extensive relationship does not yet encompass the Persian Gulf's military security arrangements—which remain exclusively with the United States, Britain, and France—and although few serious attempts have been made by either side to replace or balance these with new Pacific Asian alliances, this may change soon. Meanwhile, there is compelling evidence that the two regions are seeking to strengthen their other non-economic ties. An abundance of state-level visits, often at much higher levels than with Western powers, and a considerable number of cooperative agreements, gifts, loans, and other incentives, are undoubtedly binding these great trade partners ever closer. Moreover, with a number of future collaborations including 'hydrocarbon safekeeping', renewable energy projects, civilian nuclear power plants, and the building of a twenty-first century 'Silk Road', the trajectory of interdependence will continue to accelerate. And with a growing realization that the Pacific-Asian economies, particularly China, may recover more quickly from the global credit crunch than the Western economies[11]—thus signifying a global shift in economic weight from the West to the East[12]—the Eastwards reorientation of the Persian Gulf monarchies can only intensify.

There exists a modest number of academic books, journal articles, and working papers that cover various aspects of this relationship. In 1990, John Calabrese provided an early analysis of China's potential relationship with West Asia in an article published by *Asian Survey*,[13] and in 1991, his original analysis was updated and extended in a comprehensive book—*China's Changing Relations with the Middle East*.[14] The following year Charles Davies edited *Global Interests in the Arab Gulf*—one of the first and broadest studies of the region's international interactions,[15] with chapters by Susumu Ishida[16] and Anoushivaran Ehteshami[17] on, respectively, Japan's oil and military strategy in the Persian Gulf and the relationship between the newly industrialized Asian countries and the Gulf. At about the same time, the Xinjiang University Press published a book on the Persian Gulf in Chinese, edited by Zhang Baoguo. Entitled *Strategic Studies of Xinjiang's Opening to the Countries of Western Asia*, the book provided an early insight into possible future Chinese policies—or at least the policies of its most Muslim and most western province—with regards to the Persian Gulf.[18] Writing in 1998, Barry Rubin drew much needed attention to China's overall emerging Middle East strategy in an article for *China Report*,[19] while Calabrese provided a more specific examination of China's security and energy needs in the Persian Gulf monarchies in an article published by *Middle East Journal*.[20]

More recently there have been several additional studies on the phenomenon including the UAE scholar Muhammad bin Huwaidin's highly original book—*China's Relations with Arabia and the Gulf: 1949–1999*, published in

2002,[21] and his follow-up article on Saudi Arabia's foreign policy towards China published by the *Journal of Strategic Studies*.[22] In 2004, Ehteshami revisited the wider relationship between the Middle East and Asia with an edited volume—*The Middle East's Relations with Asia and Russia*—in cooperation with Britain's Foreign and Commonwealth Office.[23] This included a chapter on Asian geostrategic realities and their likely impact on the Middle East, including the Persian Gulf,[24] and a specific chapter on China's evolving strategy.[25] In 2007, Henry Lee and Dan Shalmon investigated China's various oil initiatives in the Middle East in their paper published by Harvard University's Belfer Center for Science and International Affairs,[26] while Steve Yetiv and Chunlong Yu provided perhaps the most succinct study to date of China's overall position in the region in their article published by *Middle East Journal*.[27]

In 2008, the Japanese scholar Yukiko Miyagi reintroduced Japan to the discussion in her innovative English language book—*Japan's Middle East Security Policy*.[28] In 2009, as interest in the linkages between the two regions continued to intensify, the Iranian scholar Mahmoud Ghafour provided an overview of China's policy towards the Persian Gulf in his article for *Middle East Policy*[29] while Calabrese published a timely and thought-provoking policy brief for Washington DC's Middle East Institute entitled *The Consolidation of Gulf-Asia Relations: Washington Tuned in or Out of Touch?*.[30] Also in 2009, David Adam Stott introduced the topic of nuclear cooperation to the scholarly debate in his article on Japan and the UAE for the *Asia-Pacific Journal*,[31] while the Royal Bank of Scotland's chief China economist, Ben Simpfendorfer, published his landmark book *The New Silk Road: How a Rising Arab World is Turning Away from the West and Rediscovering China*.[32] Not only did this study examine the many physical manifestations of the reinvigoration of this ancient trade route, but the polyglot Simpfendorfer also provided a unique portrait of the many cultural and political connections that are fast developing on both the periphery and at the core of the new China-Middle East relationship.

What few of these academic texts and policy briefings have provided, however, is a concise and specialized overview of the very specific, yet multi-polar relationship that is evolving between the Persian Gulf monarchies and the three principal Pacific Asian economies. Most of the above studies have focused on the entire Middle Eastern region, rather than distinguishing the Persian Gulf monarchies and their particular economic, social, and political characteristics from neighbouring Arab states or Iran. Moreover, with a few exceptions, the bulk of research on the East Asian side of this subject is either too broad, with little distinction being made between Asian countries that are developing at either very different paces or in very different directions, or the research is overly China-centric. Although China is undoubtedly becoming the driving force behind Asia's economic development and any future Asianisation of the continent, Japan nonetheless remains a major economic power and partner for the Persian Gulf monarchies while South Korea—as this book will demonstrate—has in some cases even overtaken its larger Pacific Asian neighbours to become the primary economic partner of certain Gulf states. A wave of recent think tank and consultancy reports have tried to address the subject, but even though many of these are highly informative, the majority are very narrow bilateral studies or are also too broad. Also, by their very nature and given the fast moving nature of the emerging Persian Gulf-Pacific Asian relationship, most are quickly outdated or become little more than brief snapshots of what is really a long-running process.

Structure of the Book

The first chapter examines the initial points of significant contact, at least in modern times, between the Persian Gulf monarchies and the Pacific Asian economies. Following a discussion of Britain's role in the Persian Gulf and its largely inhibiting effect on its various protectorates with regard to building relationships with other states, the chapter then considers Japan's historic ability to penetrate Saudi Arabia's oil industry and its increased involvement in the region's re-export trade, especially in Dubai. China's early role in the Persian Gulf is then examined, with an emphasis on re-exporting activity with Kuwait and Qatar, followed by a discussion of China's first major international oil imports in the early 1980s from the Sultanate of Oman. The second chapter continues to build up the background to the contemporary analysis by providing a brief economic and demographic comparison between the two regions. The various gross domestic products of the featured states are discussed along with their population sizes, their labour force sizes, and their respective hydrocarbon production capabilities or, in the case of the Pacific Asian economies, their increasing hydrocarbon import needs. Moreover, the principal sovereign wealth funds of both the Persian Gulf monarchies and the Pacific Asian economies are listed, along with their estimated values.

The third chapter takes a more detailed look at the hydrocarbon trade between the two regions. Following an overview of the Persian Gulf monarchies' share of global hydrocarbon production and the Pacific Asian economies' share of global hydrocarbon consumption, each of the three Pacific Asian states' linkages with their hydrocarbon suppliers are analysed. In particular, the various concessions and agreements that underpin these relationships are considered, along with the factors that may shape the future hydrocarbon trade between the two groups. Similarly, the fourth chapter addresses the growing non-hydrocarbon trade and provides data on the current levels of non-hydrocarbon imports and exports. Along with the various government-level agreements, both bilateral and multilateral, that are being put in place to facilitate this dimension of the strengthening relationship, the chapter also details the numerous other initiatives that are being introduced to improve this trade.

The fifth chapter provides a comprehensive analysis of the massive investments that are now being made—in both directions—between the Persian Gulf monarchies and the Pacific Asian economies. The chapter begins by explaining the increasing attractiveness of such an investment relationship for both groups of countries before then turning to each of the three featured Pacific Asian economies and detailing both the sovereign wealth investments and private investments that are being made, and the various joint ventures that are being set up with their Persian Gulf partners. The sixth chapter builds on this discussion by studying the increasing interdependence between the two regions in the field of construction and labour. It is demonstrated that the Pacific Asian construction companies, despite having a much shorter track record in the region than their Western or Arab competitors, are nonetheless winning an increasing share of contracts in the Persian Gulf, with South Korean companies having been particularly successful. The chapter also considers the impact of the credit crunch on the construction industry—especially in Dubai—and how this may have affected the relationship between the various Persian Gulf and Pacific Asian partners involved.

The seventh chapter tries to answer the puzzling question of why there is still no security dimension to the otherwise tightening relationship between the two regions. Following a brief discussion of earlier Pacific Asian involvement in the Persian Gulf's security arrangements, including the various political obstacles that have had to be overcome, the chapter proceeds to detail the continuing Western military presence in the region, before explaining why—despite a few recent indications of change—the Pacific Asian economies for the most part remain either unable or unwilling to modify the existing situation. The eighth chapter is also, in some ways, an answer to this question, as it demonstrates that even though a military security arrangement between the two regions does not yet exist, there is nonetheless increasing evidence of an extensive range of other non-economic linkages forming. Most notably, the chapter identifies the increasing frequency and seniority of state-level diplomatic visits between the Persian Gulf monarchies and the Pacific Asian economies, along with the various aid packages and cultural and educational exchanges that have only recently begun to take place.

The ninth and final chapter, which is perhaps this book's most original contribution, is a study of some of the most notable future initiatives and collaborations that are soon likely to take place between the two groups of countries and will certainly increase their interdependency even further. In particular, it is shown how some of the Pacific Asian economies will begin to serve as proxy hydrocarbon reserves for their Persian Gulf partners: a mutually beneficial arrangement that has significant economic, logistical, and security implications. The chapter then demonstrates how the Pacific Asian economies will soon assume a leading role in the fast growing renewable energy sector in the Persian Gulf, before discussing how the physical trade links between the two regions are likely to improve following the construction of new pan-Asian highways and deep water ports. Finally, the chapter examines the greatest and most symbolic future partnership that is developing: South Korea's winning of a massive contract to construct and maintain the United Arab Emirates' nuclear power plants over the next several decades. With at least some of the UAE's Persian Gulf neighbours also considering setting up civilian nuclear industries, the opportunities for further Pacific Asian involvement will be enormous.

Further Notes

In the various charts and tables featured throughout this book, the six Persian Gulf monarchies will be listed according to their gross domestic product, beginning with Saudi Arabia (with the highest GDP) and ending with Bahrain (with the lowest GDP). The three featured Pacific Asian economies will also be listed according to their GDP, although for the most part Japan will still be placed ahead of China given its longer history of ties with the Persian Gulf and its position of economic preeminence until very recently. Undoubtedly if this book were being written in 2012 rather than 2009, then China would have been placed ahead of Japan. This book also contains a number of words that have been transliterated from Arabic, Japanese, Chinese languages or Korean. These are mostly place names and the names of various businesspeople, politicians, or other dignitaries. These have been transliterated according to their most popular spelling in English; however I apologise in advance for any minor inconsistencies that may result.

1

HISTORICAL BACKGROUND

The oil trade between the Persian Gulf monarchies and the Pacific Asian states began much later than that between the Gulf and the Western powers, with both Bahrain and Kuwait having begun exporting to Britain in the 1930s. By the early 1950s, however, Tokyo oil companies were beginning to scour the globe for resources to fuel Japan's rapid post-war industrialisation programme, following a short and unsatisfactory period of domestic coal production.[1] Most of the Gulf sheikhdoms, including Bahrain, Qatar, and Abu Dhabi were off limits at this time to Japan, as they were not independent states and remained very much a part of Britain's 'Trucial System'—a series of perpetually renewed nineteenth-century peace treaties that had been signed between London and the indigenous ruling families. The treaties guaranteed British protection for the sheikhs in exchange for exclusive imperial control over all political and economic relations involving their territories.[2] The hinterland of the Arabian Peninsula, however, was the key exception, with Britain having failed to install a robust ruler sympathetic to imperial interests in the 1920s and therefore having had little option but to recognise formally King Abdul-Aziz bin Saud's independent rule over his conquests in 1932. Britain's Iraqi Petroleum Company was thus unable to prevent the United States' Standard Oil of California from commencing exploration the following year, and in 1953 the Japanese government was able to dispatch freely an economic delegation to Saudi Arabia, with formal diplomatic relations between Tokyo and Riyadh beginning soon after. By 1956, Japan's Arabian Oil Company had secured a forty-three-year concession to explore and extract Saudi oil from the neutral zone between Saudi Arabia and Kuwait,[3] and in 1961 production facilities were finally established.[4] The lucrative relationship was then quickly strengthened by the Saudi ruling family, with its first ever minister for defence—Prince Sultan bin Abdul-Aziz Al-Saud—visiting Tokyo in 1960, and with its third ruler, King Faisal bin Abdul-Aziz Al-Saud, visiting in 1971.[5] By this stage, nearly 65 per cent of Japan's energy supply was coming from oil, and much of this was being imported from Saudi Arabia.[6]

In parallel to the foothold that its oil companies were establishing, the non-hydrocarbon trade between the Persian Gulf monarchies and Japan was also beginning to flourish, although its origins were rather more circuitous. Dubai, although one of the Trucial States,[7] had long been exploring inventive ways of circumventing Britain's tight economic controls,[8] and, by building on its much documented history as a regional entrepôt, in the 1950s and 1960s the sheikh-dom managed to position itself as the primary re-export hub for goods destined for India.[9] Following the latter's independence from the British Empire and the attempts of its first prime minister, Jawaharlal Nehru, to replicate the Soviet miracle by using the state to plan and protect the economy, a number of restrictive practices were introduced that effectively prevented India-based merchants from meeting domestic demand for their products, especially fabrics. In particular, sasooni cotton from the Nichibo mills in Japan was in great demand, along with cotton latha from the Nishinbo Three Peaches and Toyobo Flying Dragon mills. Dubai played the role of an intermediary, with its merchants carefully ordering the necessary materials well in advance so as to overcome the lengthy five-month shipping time from Japan. Similarly profitable was Dubai's trade in sourcing specialist textiles such as Japan's Tetron for wealthy Indians and Pakistanis resident in both Dubai and Bombay, often for use in the manufacture of saris and other garments.[10] By the late 1970s, Dubai's trade with Japan had expanded to include electrical goods, with the re-exporting of millions of Hitachi personal stereos to the subcontinent,[11] and by 1982 thousands of Japanese television sets were being distributed across India and the Persian Gulf,[12] with demand being catalysed by Delhi's hosting of the Asian Games that year.[13]

With Britain's granting of independence to Kuwait in 1961, and with the dismantling of the Trucial States system in 1971, Japan's opportunities for further oil concessions and more formal non-hydrocarbon trade expanded to include all of the Persian Gulf monarchies. Formal diplomatic relations were duly established with Kuwait in 1961, and in late 1971, Japan was one of the first states to recognise the newly formed seven member federation of United Arab Emirates. The following year relations were also established with the Sultanate of Oman and with the two newly independent emirates of Qatar and Bahrain, both of which had chosen to remain outside of the UAE for political and economic reasons.[14] The Arabian Oil Company—by this stage 80 per cent owned by Japan and 20 per cent owned by Saudi Arabia and Kuwait—was therefore able to build on its original concession in Saudi Arabia and promptly signed a concession in Kuwait in 1961.[15] As a condition of this concession, in 1967 the Arabian Oil Company deepened its relationship with Kuwait by co-establishing with the Kuwaiti government the Kuwait Institute for Scientific Research (KISR). Tasked with launching research projects in the fields of petroleum, desert agriculture, and marine biology, the institute was supported in its early endeavours by a team of Japanese experts, and in 1973 it was formally integrated into the Kuwaiti government.[16] Later that year, the Japanese Oil Development Company (JODCO) successfully negotiated a stake in an international consortium to exploit a UAE offshore oil concession.[17]

In support of these booming hydrocarbon and non-hydrocarbon trades with the Persian Gulf, it is no coincidence that Japan's share of official development assistance (ODA) destined for the region began to increase dramatically during this period. By 1975, following the oil price crisis of 1973–1974, Japan's ODA to the Middle East (mostly for the Gulf) accounted for over 10 per cent of its total or about $90 million, compared to just 2 per cent at the beginning of the decade. By the late 1970s, nearly a quarter of ODA or about $220 million was being allocated to the region, before the share began to settle back to about 10 per cent for the duration of the 1980s, being worth about $580 million in 1988.[18]

Although China had been involved in some of the re-export trade in the Persian Gulf since the late nineteenth century, the volume was understandably low due to the Trucial States system.[19] Moreover, following the establishment of the People's Republic of China in 1949, policymakers in Beijing largely ignored the Persian Gulf monarchies on the grounds that they were 'either under British colonial rule or ruled by reactionary monarchs closely allied with the West...thus the Western grip was strong enough to influence the direction of their foreign policies in favour of the West.' By the mid-1950s, with many of the Gulf sheikhs having condemned China as the aggressor in the recent Korean War, criticizing China for the subjugation of its Muslim population, and preferring to recognize Taiwan as the legitimate Chinese state, the position of the People's Republic in the region was limited even further.[20] Most of its trade links were confined to Qatar and Kuwait, rather than the increasingly prosperous Dubai.[21] As such, between 1950 and 1955 it was estimated that

Table 1.1: Early Japanese official development assistance to the Persian Gulf as a share of total Japanese ODA (millions of US dollars)

Year	Total ODA	Persian Gulf ODA	As a percentage
1960–1969	1938.7	7.9	0.4
1971	432.1	4.9	1.2
1973	765.2	10.6	1.4
1975	850.4	90.4	10.6
1977	899.3	219.9	24.5
1979	1921.2	203.5	10.6
1981	2260.4	190.1	8.4
1983	2425.2	200.5	8.3
1985	2556.9	201.1	7.9
1987	5247.9	526.1	10.1

Source: Japanese Ministry for Foreign Affairs.

Chinese trade with the Persian Gulf amounted to less than $1.7 million per annum, which was barely half a per cent of its total world trade.[22] With sizeable domestic hydrocarbon reserves and less momentum behind its industrialisation programme, China's interest in an oil trade with the Persian Gulf monarchies was much slower to develop than Japan's. Moreover, as will be discussed later in this book,[23] during this Maoist period in which China was closely aligned with the Union of Soviet Socialist Republics (USSR)[24] and was openly supporting anti-imperialist, revolutionary movements, China was effectively stymieing most of its opportunities for closer ties with the Gulf's ruling families,[25] most of which were fearful of Arab nationalist or Soviet-backed uprisings and—with the exception of independent Saudi Arabia—preferred not to upset their British guarantors.

Nonetheless there were some signs of improving relations. In 1956, Saudi Arabia permitted Chinese Muslims to enter the kingdom for the purposes of performing the *hajj* pilgrimage. Between 1956 and 1959, several Chinese cultural delegations were dispatched to Saudi Arabia, and by 1960 Chinese trade with the region had increased to $34 million per annum—about 1 per cent of its total world trade.[26] In 1961, immediately following Kuwait's independence from Britain, China seized the opportunity to strengthen its foothold, with an official communiqué being delivered to the new government wishing the 'people of Kuwait further successes in the cause of opposing imperialism and colonialism, safeguarding national independence and building their country.'[27] With an eye on the future, the pioneering ruler of Kuwait, Sheikh Abdullah Al-Salim Al-Sabah, even made the bold step of visiting China in 1965. And in 1971, with the coming to power of a more open-minded Chinese president—Zhou Enlai—full diplomatic relations were put in place between the two countries, thus marking China's first official link to the region.[28] Kuwait was undoubtedly viewed by China as a potential stepping-stone to the other Persian Gulf monarchies.[29] And it is likely that China held a particularly favourable view of Kuwait given that it had nationalised its oil industry, thus abolishing Western-held concessions. Also, with the Al-Sabah ruling family doing little to disguise its distrust of the USSR, China made the most of a shared common enemy, as this was a time when rivalry between China and the USSR was growing.[30] Certainly, Beijing newspapers began to report regularly on anti-Soviet statements in the Kuwaiti media, including Kuwait's criticism of 'the Soviet Union opening the door for the emigration of Jews to Palestine', and 'the Kuwaiti press exposing the scandalous acts of the Soviet Union in making fabulous profits by reselling oil obtained from the Arab region to western Europe... thus refuting the Soviet nonsense about the oil in the Gulf being international property... which aimed at legalising Soviet plunder of Gulf oil.'[31]

By 1978 circumstances were continuing to improve. A 'cultural revolution'[32] that had been gripping China for the best part of a decade and had led to a resurgence in the persecution of its Muslim population had finally come to an end. Moreover, total trade between China and the Persian Gulf monarchies had reached in excess of $180 million, most of which was with Kuwait,[33] and the initiation of a series of Chinese economic and political reforms—the 'Four Modernisations'—that aimed to stimulate economic growth and support modernisation[34] had effectively led to a rapid downgrading of Marxist ideologies in China's external relations.[35] With this obstacle removed and the door opened to previously inconceivable strategic alliances,[36] Oman immediately established diplomatic relations with China while the UAE followed suit in 1984.[37] The following year Saudi Arabia held its first official meeting with China on Omani territory,[38] when its Crown Prince met with the Chinese vice-president on the premise of celebrating Oman's national day.[39] The Qataris also present at this event, and invited a Chinese delegation to visit Doha the following year, under the guise of the eighteenth anniversary of the Red Crescent and Red Cross Societies. Reportedly, the Chinese were delighted to learn that Qatar had followed Kuwait's lead by also nationalising its oil industry.[40]

Moreover, just days after the 1981 formation of the Gulf Cooperation Council (GCC)—the loose organisation that was to represent the joint interests of the Persian Gulf monarchies—China had granted it full recognition.[41] The formalisation of relations with the UAE was in many ways inevitable, as successful trade missions between the two countries had already commenced in 1978, and since 1980 Chinese civilian airlines had been using Sharjah's airport as their primary refueling base en route to European and African destinations.[42] Upon exchanging ambassadors with Oman, China's newspapers attempted to rewrite their country's history of supporting revolutionary movements in southern Arabia by stating that 'Oman suffered historically from aggression and oppression by imperialism and colonialism in order to achieve national independence...today the Omani government is dedicating its efforts to the struggle in defence of national independence and for the development of the national economy.'[43] Oman's minister of state for foreign affairs was then dispatched to Beijing to be warned by the Chinese president that the USSR intended to expand its influence in the region and that '...bloated with wild ambition, the superpower flaunting the signboard of "socialism" is making trouble everywhere and stepping up all-round expansion in an attempt to place the area under its control.'[44] In 1983, another important forward step took place when China took the decision to begin importing crude oil from Oman, the only Persian Gulf monarchy that was able to ship oil from Indian Ocean ports and thus save Chinese tankers from having to sail into the Gulf via the Strait of Hormuz. This arrangement was originally viewed by Beijing as being a temporary measure that would alleviate the problem of transporting Chinese oil from the northern provinces to refineries on the Yangtze River. There was, it would seem, every intention that internal transportation difficulties would be eventually solved and that Omani imports could be curtailed. However, by 1988, as Chinese demand for oil was accelerating rapidly in tandem with its increasing population and intensifying industrialisation, the Omani arrangement was made permanent.[45]

At the same time that these early Chinese oil interests were developing in the region, China's predominantly Muslim provinces—the five northwestern territories of Xingjian, Gansu, Qinghai, Ningxia, and Shaanxi—were also beginning to connect to the Persian Gulf, albeit independently from the Beijing government. As effectively semi-autonomous provinces, they began to send individual delegations (including political and business leaders as well as religious figures and medical personnel)[46] to Saudi Arabia and Kuwait on the grounds that these Gulf states were more suitable and more proximate trade and investment partners for Chinese Muslim businessmen than Japanese or European companies were. Notably, Xinjiang dispatched a 'friendship delegation' to Riyadh and Mecca in 1985, which met with both the Saudi grand mufti and the minister for defence,[47] and followed up by hosting an 'overseas economic and trade fair' for Saudi visitors later that year. In 1986, a Xinjiang delegation also visited the UAE emirate of Sharjah, to meet with both its ruler—Sheikh Sultan bin Muhammad Al-Qasimi—and officials from the Sharjah Chamber of Commerce and Industry. Reportedly, both religious issues and potential trade collaborations were discussed.[48] Shortly after, Saudi Arabia donated a million copies of the Koran to Xinjiang, while the Jeddah-based Islamic Development Bank donated about $4 million to Xinjiang and Ningxia to improve their existing Islamic academies and to help set up Arabic language schools. The five provinces later hosted a tour of the Kuwait Religious Foundation,[49] and in 1988, the relationship tightened further between Ningxia and Saudi Arabia following the joint establishment of a new investment company—the Al-Barakah-Ningxia Islamic International Trust—in Ningxia's principal city.[50]

By end of the decade the Beijing government had reasserted its leadership in developing China's links with the Persian Gulf, with China's official presence soon extending to all of the monarchies, at least on the diplomatic front, with embassies being set up in Qatar in 1988, in Bahrain in 1989, and finally in Saudi Arabia in 1990.[51] Importantly, the latter mission was made possible following King Fahd bin Abdul-Aziz Al-Saud's decision to downgrade Saudi Arabia's existing relations with Taiwan, thus supporting China's insistence that its allies adhered to a 'One China' policy.[52] In fact, Saudi Arabia's embassy in Taipei was re-designated as a 'representative office,'[53] in order to avoid severing Taiwanese relations completely. Clearly, Fahd had determined that the potential strategic importance of China, not least its permanent membership of the United Nations Security Council, greatly outweighed Saudi Arabia's more principled existing relationship with Taipei.[54] But in many ways the exchanging of ambassadors between China and Saudi Arabia was by this stage little more than a formality, as many analysts argued that the other Persian Gulf monarchies were unlikely to have formalised their relations with China without some degree of Saudi consent. Moreover, the two countries had already established commercial representative offices in each other's capital cities in 1988, both of which were situated in embassy districts.[55] A missile deal had already been concluded between Riyadh and Beijing—as discussed later in this book[56]—and there were frequent reports of Saudi individuals having visited China throughout the decade, all of whom had presumably gained the tacit consent of the Riyadh government.[57] Significantly, by this stage there were also 2,000 Chinese Muslims undertaking annual pilgrimages to Mecca and Medina.[58]

South Korea was far less proactive than Japan and China during this period, with its major oil companies not having been established until the late 1970s[59]—during the boom years of the Fourth Republic—and with most of its other trade links with the Persian Gulf monarchies also having developed more recently. Nonetheless, a modest 10 per cent of South Korea's manufacturing exports were destined for the Persian Gulf in the 1970s[60]—mostly basic construction materials—and discussions began with Saudi Arabia to construct a crude oil terminal and storage depot on South Korea's southern coastline as part of a $350 million joint venture.[61] Although the latter project stalled, South Korea was nonetheless building up the foundations of its presently strong political relationship with the region, with its president, Choi Kyu-Hah, making a full tour of the Persian Gulf in 1980.[62] For the most part, South Korea established diplomatic relations with the Persian Gulf monarchies in the wake of Japan, but ahead of China, with embassies being set up in Saudi Arabia in 1961, in Oman in 1974, in Qatar in 1974, in Bahrain in 1976, in Kuwait in 1979, and finally in the UAE in 1980.[63]

Table 1.2: Establishing diplomatic missions, 1954–1990

	Japan	China	South Korea
Saudi Arabia	1954	1990	1961
UAE	1971	1984	1980
Kuwait	1961	1971	1979
Qatar	1972	1988	1974
Oman	1972	1978	1974
Bahrain	1972	1989	1976

Sources: Japanese, Chinese, and South Korean Ministries for Foreign Affairs.

2

ECONOMIC AND DEMOGRAPHIC COMPARISON

With rapidly expanding economies and, in some cases, rapidly expanding populations, accurate and timely statistics for the Persian Gulf monarchies and the leading Pacific-Asia economies are difficult to compile and are soon dated. Nonetheless, a compilation of the presently available data still serves as a useful snapshot of the ever-increasing compatibility and congruency of the two regions and helps to understand the current trajectory of their relationship. Most noticeably, since trade links and formal diplomatic relations were first established between the majority of these countries in the 1960s and 1970s, most of the Persian Gulf monarchies have since confirmed their position as the world's leading hydrocarbon exporters, with a plethora of recent discoveries and a commitment to building the most extensive oil and gas infrastructure in the world guaranteeing increased export capacity for the foreseeable future. Moreover, over the same period most of these monarchies have been carefully investing their hydrocarbon export surpluses in massive state-managed sovereign wealth funds, all of which are seeking access to new markets and opportunities.

Equally clear is that Japan remains one of the world's largest economies, despite suffering nearly two 'lost decades' of recession and low growth following the dramatic crash of Japanese asset prices in 1991.[1] Over the same period, China's economic growth has captivated the world, prompting talk of a 'Chinese century' that will follow on from the United States' twentieth century and Britain's nineteenth century.[2] Indeed, over the past few years China has caught up with Japan's gross domestic product and in 2009, it even eclipsed the original Asian tiger economy, with a GDP growth rate of nearly 8 per cent[3] despite the international slow down following the global credit crunch. Although with a much smaller economy than its neighbours, South Korea's growth has been consistently good, and its GDP now exceeds that of many Western industrialised economies, with a very respectable GDP per capita of nearly $30,000. To keep up with this phenomenal growth, the reliance of the Pacific Asian economies on hydrocarbon fuels has increased drastically, the bulk of which now has to be imported. In China's case, there has also been a population explosion, especially in the early 1970s,[4] and as a result its labour force has now mushroomed to several hundred million, making opportunities for the overseas employment of Chinese nationals increasingly vital. As with the Persian Gulf monarchies, Japan's potential to make sizeable foreign investments remains strong, but even more notable is the recent emergence of large state managed funds in China and South Korea, some of which have already begun to eclipse their Persian Gulf counterparts and are now responsible for administering hundreds of billions of dollars of sovereign wealth.

Chart 2.1: GDP of Japan, China, and South Korea (billions of US dollars)

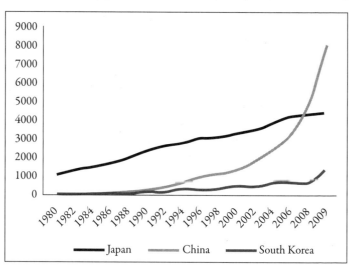

Sources: Chinese National Bureau of Statistics, Organization for Economic Cooperation and Development, International Monetary Fund.[5]

Table 2.1: Persian Gulf and Pacific Asian economic and demographic overview, 2009

Country	GDP	GDP/Capita	Resident Population	Labour Force
Japan	$4.3 trillion	$34,200	127.0 million	66.2 million
China	$7.8 trillion	$6,000	1338.6 million	807.7 million
South Korea	$1.3 trillion	$26,000	45.5 million	24.4 million
Saudi Arabia	$0.6 trillion	$20,700	28.6 million (*20% expatriates*)	6.7 million
UAE	$0.2 trillion	$40,000	4.8 million (*86% expatriates*)	3.3 million
Kuwait	$0.2 trillion	$57,400	2.7 million (*48% expatriates*)	2.2 million
Qatar	$0.1 trillion	$103,500	0.8 million (*80% expatriates*)	1.1 million
Oman	$0.1 trillion	$20,200	3.4 million (*17% expatriates*)	0.9 million
Bahrain	> $0.1 trillion	$37,200	0.7 million (*32% expatriates*)	0.5 million

Sources: CIA World Factbook, International Monetary Fund, World Bank, Organization for Economic Cooperation and Development.[6]

Table 2.2: Persian Gulf and Pacific Asian hydrocarbon demand and reserves, 2009

Country	Oil Reserves	Oil Consumed	Gas Reserves	Gas Consumed
Japan	> 0.1 billion barrels	5.0 million barrels/day (100% imported)	> 0.01 trillion cubic metres	100.3 billion cubic metres/year (96% imported)
China	16.0 billion barrels	7.9 million barrels/day (58% imported)	2.3 trillion cubic metres	70.5 billion cubic metres/year (5% imported)
South Korea	0	2.1 million barrels/day (100% imported)	0.1 trillion cubic metres	37.0 billion cubic metres/year (93% imported)
Saudi Arabia	266.8 billion barrels	1.0 million barrels/day	7.2 trillion cubic metres	75.9 billion cubic metres/year
UAE	97.8 billion barrels	0.4 million barrels/day	6.1 trillion cubic metres	43.1 billion cubic metres/year (3% imported)
Kuwait	104.0 billion barrels	0.3 million barrels/day	1.6 trillion cubic metres	12.5 billion cubic metres/year
Qatar	15.2 billion barrels	0.1 million barrels/day	25.6 trillion cubic metres	20.1 billion cubic metres/year
Oman	5.5 billion barrels	0.1 million barrels/day	0.1 trillion cubic metres	11.0 billion cubic metres/year
Bahrain	0.1 billion barrels	> 0.1 million barrels/day (50% imported)	0.1 trillion cubic metres	11.3 billion cubic metres/year

Sources: CIA World Factbook, International Monetary Fund, World Bank, Organization for Economic Cooperation and Development.[7]

Table 2.3: Persian Gulf and Pacific Asian sovereign wealth funds by assets under management, 2009

Rank	Fund name	Country	Date of inception	Origin of wealth	Current assets
1	Abu Dhabi Investment Authority	UAE (Abu Dhabi)	1976	Oil surpluses	$627 billion
2	SAMA Foreign Holdings	Saudi Arabia	1960	Oil surpluses	$431 billion
4	SAFE Investment Company	China	1997	Non-hydrocarbon	$347 billion
5	China Investment Corporation	China	2007	Non-hydrocarbon	$288 billion
7	Kuwait Investment Authority	Kuwait	1963	Oil surpluses	$203 billion
8	Hong Kong Monetary Policy Investment Portfolio	China (Hong Kong)	1998	Non-hydrocarbon	$193 billion
11	National Social Security Fund	China	2000	Non-hydrocarbon	$82 billion
12	Investment Corporation of Dubai	UAE (Dubai)	2006	Oil surpluses	$82 billion
14	Qatar Investment Authority	Qatar	2006	Gas surpluses	$65 billion
20	Korea Investment Corporation	South Korea	2005	Non-hydrocarbon	$27 billion
25	Mubadala Development Corporation	UAE (Abu Dhabi)	2002	Non-hydrocarbon	$15 billion
26	Mumtalakat Holding Company	Bahrain	2006	Oil surpluses	$14 billion
27	International Petroleum Investment Company	UAE (Abu Dhabi)	1984	Oil surpluses	$14 billion
35	State General Reserve Fund	Oman	1980	Oil and gas surpluses	$8 billion

Sources: Sovereign Wealth Fund Institute, Saudi Arabia Market Information Resource and Directory.[8]

3

THE HYDROCARBON TRADE

The supply and demand of oil and gas undoubtedly remains the central pillar in the relationship between the Persian Gulf monarchies and the Pacific Asian economies, and their total hydrocarbon trade could now be worth as much as $192.2 billion per annum.[1] It is important to note that the Pacific Asian economies do little to disguise their dependency on hydrocarbon imports from the Persian Gulf, in contrast to many of the Western powers, most of which are openly trying to reduce their dependency and diversify their sources. Indeed, the United States has a stated policy favouring the diversification of its oil supply and is actively working to promote oil production in countries outside of the Middle East.[2] In early 2010, Canada even overtook Saudi Arabia to become the US' primary supplier of oil following heavy US investment in developing the Athabasca Tar Sands. Soon Angola, Nigeria, and Brazil may also displace Saudi Arabia as a top US supplier, while in the longer term the Caspian Sea's offshore hydrocarbon deposits are viewed as another good alternative to the Persian Gulf.[3] US demand has also fallen, with imports of crude oil having peaked in 2005 at 10 million barrels per day, and with demand having fallen by nine per cent in both 2008 and 2009 in the wake of the global credit crunch.[4] In contrast, the Pacific Asian economies appear to have few problems in portraying themselves as reliable customers that are entering into a mutually dependent relationship with their hydrocarbon suppliers.[5] If anything, they are clearly seeking every opportunity to intensify their hydrocarbon trade links with the Persian Gulf monarchies, while simultaneously building up several other areas of mutual interest, as outlined in the latter chapters of this book.

At present, the Persian Gulf monarchies produce a combined total of about 16.6 billion barrels of crude oil per day,[6] which is about 19 per cent of the global total. The bulk of this production takes place in Saudi Arabia, the United Arab Emirates, and Kuwait. The region also produces about 232 billion cubic metres of natural gas per year,[7] which is about 8 per cent of the global total. The bulk of this production takes place in Qatar, Saudi Arabia, and the UAE. But more importantly, perhaps, the Persian Gulf monarchies account for 37 per cent of all known crude oil reserves and 25 per cent of all known natural gas reserves.[8] Certainly, with Saudi Arabia alone accounting for 25 per cent of global oil reserves[9] and with Qatar accounting for at least 15 per cent of global gas reserves[10]—the bulk of which is extracted from its giant offshore North Field, shared with Iran—the region will remain central to the global energy industry for several more decades.

At the other extreme, Japan's current hydrocarbon consumption is 5 million barrels of oil per day, 100 per cent of which it has to import, and 100.3 billion cubic metres of gas per year, 95 per cent of which it has to import. Since the Tokyo government retreated to a secondary role in Japan's energy industry in the 1990s and allowed the market to take over the country's oil purchases, various energy companies in Japan have arranged much of these imports.[11] Although China is relatively more self sufficient, its rapidly accelerating consumption of oil—which currently stands at about 7.9 million barrels of oil per

Chart 3.1: Global share of oil production, 2009

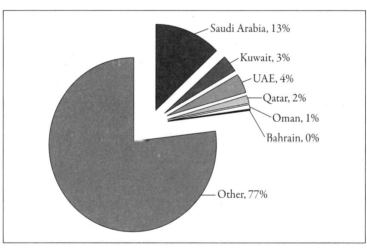

Sources: EIA; CIA World Factbook.[12]

Chart 3.2: Global share of oil reserves, 2009

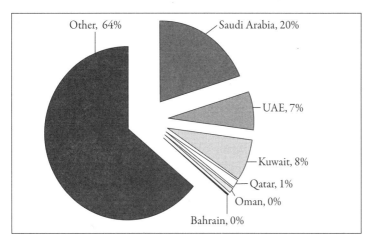

Sources: EIA; CIA World Factbook.[13]

Chart 3.3: Global share of natural gas reserves, 2009

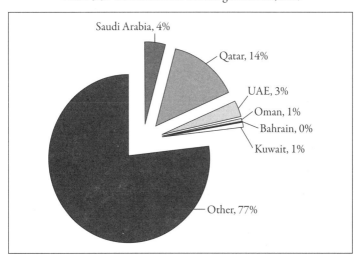

Sources: EIA; CIA World Factbook.[14]

day and rose by an incredible 14 per cent in 2009[15]—nonetheless means that the country already has to import 58 per cent of its needs. And with gas consumption at 70.5 billion cubic metres per year, 5 per cent of its gas now has to be imported, despite China being one of the world's top ten gas producers[16] and despite it having made several large indigenous discoveries in recent years.[17] In comparison, South Korea's hydrocarbon needs are more modest, given the smaller size of its economy and population, but with oil consumption now at 2.1 million barrels per day and with gas consumption at 37 billion cubic metres of gas per year, its dependency will soon be as acute as Japan's. Indeed, 100 per cent of South Korea's oil is already being imported, whilst 93 per cent of its gas is imported. Unlike Japan, Chinese and South Korean hydrocarbon imports are still arranged by giant, state-owned companies and bilateral government-to-government agreements.[18]

Respectively, China and Japan have the second and third greatest oil consumption needs in the world, behind only the US and now ahead of India, Russia, and Germany. Significantly, South Korea has now also entered into the top ten. Japan has the fifth greatest gas consumption needs in the world, ahead of Germany and Britain, while China and South Korea have now moved into the top twenty,[19] and are likely to catch and overtake Japan in the near future.

Chart 3.4: Global oil consumption, 2009 (millions of barrels per day)

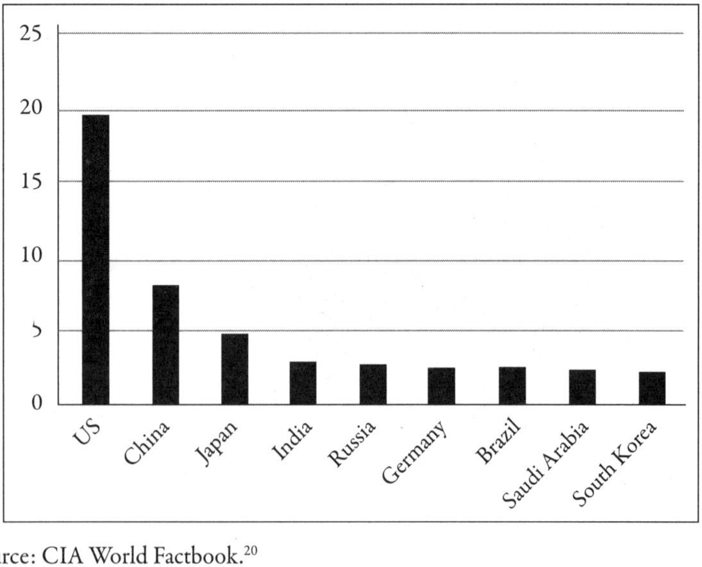

Source: CIA World Factbook.[20]

Chart 3.5: Global natural gas consumption, 2009
(billions of cubic metres per year)

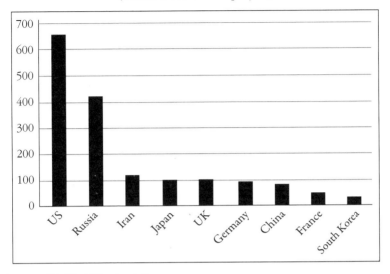

Source: CIA World Factbook.[21]

Certainly, according to the Organization of Petroleum Exporting Countries (OPEC), although Japan's demand for oil is likely to fall by 15 per cent by 2030, China, South Korea, and other Pacific Asian economies are likely to make up 80 per cent of net global oil demand growth over the same period.[22]

The vast bulk of Japan's oil imports continue to be sourced from the Persian Gulf monarchies. Although there were some attempts in the 1970s to diversify geographically the sources of oil by purchasing from Mexico, Canada, and parts of Europe, these only ever accounted for a small share. Similarly, in the 1980s, other Asian countries such as Indonesia, Malaysia, and Brunei failed to increase their oil supplies to Japan, while African countries such as Egypt, Libya, Nigeria, and Algeria actually decreased their supplies to Japan, and the Union of Soviet Socialist Republics supplied only marginal oil exports to Japan.[23] Japan currently imports about 1.3 million barrels of oil per day from Saudi Arabia, which is over 31 per cent of its total oil imports (having risen from 24 per cent in 2008)[24] and worth close to $33 billion per year for Saudi Arabia.[25] This now makes Japan Saudi Arabia's greatest hydrocarbon trading partner,[26] with it having overtaken the US at some point in 2009. In a close second place, the UAE now exports 800,000 barrels of oil per day to Japan,[27] with total oil and gas exports from Abu Dhabi—by far the most resource-rich

Table 3.1: Persian Gulf and Pacific Asian total value of annual
hydrocarbon trade, 2009

	Japan	*China*	*South Korea*	*TOTAL*
Saudi Arabia	$33 billion	$15 billion	$21 billion	$69 billion
UAE	$47 billion	$4.5 billion	$13 billion	$64.5 billion
Kuwait	$15 billion	$0.7 billion	$8.1 billion	$23.8 billion
Qatar	$17 billion	$1 billion	$7 billion	$25 billion
Oman	$2.6 billion	$1.5 billion	$5.1 billion	$9.2 billion
Bahrain	$0.4 billion	–	$0.3 billion	$0.7 billion
TOTAL	$115 billion	$22.7 billion	$54.5 billion	$192.2 billion

Sources: CIA World Factbook; British Petroleum Statistical Review.[28]

of the UAE's seven constituent emirates[29]—now worth over $47 billion.[30] Although 800,000 barrels now only represents 22 per cent of Japan's total oil imports, down from 25 per cent in 2008, the drop can be explained by Japanese companies presently holding more favourable concessions in Saudi Arabia at a time when Japan's total oil imports dropped by 28 per cent in one year, or 278,000 barrels per day.[31] Nonetheless, the UAE may soon overtake Saudi Arabia to resume its status as Japan's primary supplier as a result of massive export capacity building in Abu Dhabi[32] and a number of recent agreements. Indeed, over 60 per cent of Abu Dhabi's oil exports are still destined for Japan,[33] and in early 2009, the Abu Dhabi National Oil Company (ADNOC) strengthened the connection further by granting a twenty-year extension to an existing offshore concession managed by a consortium led by Japan's Cosmo Oil Company.[34] This concession was originally due to expire in 2012, but was extended three years ahead of schedule as a reward for Japan signing an important nuclear technology transfer agreement with Abu Dhabi, as discussed later in this book.[35] In contrast, most of the Western companies with concessions in Abu Dhabi (the majority of which expire in 2012 or 2013) are being made to wait until the very end of their concession period before being allowed to negotiate for renewal.[36] Abu Dhabi's primary gas customer for many years has been Japan, and in particular the Tokyo Electricity Power Company (TEPCO), which purchases over 4 million tons of liquid natural gas annually from Abu Dhabi Gas Liquefaction (ADGAS), which is a subsidiary of ADNOC.[37] As something of an insight into this important relationship, in 1997 it was reported that TEPCO even paid ADGAS a one-off 'goodwill gesture' fee of

$400 million, as Japan sought to stabilise Abu Dhabi's gas revenues during a period of depressed gas prices during the late 1990s and presumably hoped to maintain its position as Abu Dhabi's preferred customer.[38] Japan's hydrocarbon trade with the other Persian Gulf monarchies is much more modest, but still noteworthy, with its annual imports from Qatar—most of which is gas—totaling $17 billion in 2008, with its imports from Kuwait—most of which is oil—totaling $15 billion, and with its imports from Oman and Bahrain being $2.6 billion and $0.4 billion respectively.[39]

China's total hydrocarbon trade with the Persian Gulf monarchies is substantially less than Japan's, mainly due to its still sizeable domestic gas reserves. Nonetheless, its oil imports from the region have been rising sharply, with $1.5 billion of imports in 1991, $20 billion in 2004, and nearly $33.8 billion in 2005.[40] In part, this is due to the flat or declining production from China's native oilfields in Daqing and Shengli, and due to the relatively minor new discoveries that have been made in recent years in the Junggar and Tarim basins.[41] Earlier boasts by Chinese officials that the Tarim basin 'has the larg-

Chart 3.6: Japan's oil imports, 2009

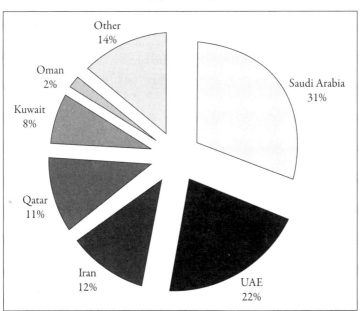

Source: Japanese Ministry for Foreign Affairs.[42]

est oil storage structure so far discovered in the world today' have proven unsubstantiated, and most international analysts have produced much lower estimates of China's oil reserves than Chinese analysts.[43] Unsurprisingly therefore, China's tenth five year plan (2001–2005) contained its government's first public acknowledgement that overseas oil supplies must be secured if China is to enjoy continued economic growth and modernisation,[44] while the eleventh five year plan (2006–2010) made the situation even more explicit. In 2001, statements were also made by China's State Petroleum and Chemical Administration that the country 'will have to strengthen its cooperation with other countries in oil-gas development, so that it can obtain abroad 50 million tons of oil and some 50 billion cubic metres of natural gas.'[45] It is also clear that few experts still believe that China can ever achieve energy self-sufficiency, even if it aggressively invests in domestic hydrocarbon production.[46] Certainly, within the next few years China's imports are likely to double once again, with one Chinese official recently admitting in a public statement that 'we need to find oil fast'[47] while another commentator has explained that 'if China's demand for oil imports was limited to just two or three million barrels per day, most of this could be sourced from Russia or nearby Central Asian republics, but with the huge oil and gas imports predicted for the next decade and beyond, China is now compelled to turn to the Persian Gulf.'[48] Certainly, the International Energy Agency (IEA) predicts that China's imports will grow to over eleven million barrels per day by 2030, more than half of which will have to be sourced from the Persian Gulf,[49] while others estimate that China will soon be importing 70 per cent of its oil from the Gulf states.[50] And although China's new gas finds are expected to keep China's gas production rate increasing by 3.1 per cent every year over the next twenty years, it is still predicted that by 2030 over a third of its gas will have to be imported.[51] As such, its current position as only the world's 35th greatest gas importer[52] will soon change.

Saudi Arabia is currently China's greatest supplier of oil, with about 1.2 million barrels of oil per day—or 30 per cent of China's total oil imports[53]—being shipped by the close of 2009, up from 843,000 barrels per day in 2008 and 500,000 barrels per day in 2007.[54] This compares to 17.5 per cent of China's total oil imports being sourced from Saudi Arabia in 2005 and just 1.2 per cent in 1994.[55] Importantly, as with Japan, in 2009 China also overtook the US as a major oil customer for Saudi Arabia. This development was believed to have prompted an end to Saudi Arabia's long running one dollar discount on oil exported to the US,[56] with one former US State Department official stating that 'Saudi Arabia used to be very much an American story, but those days are gone forever. That's just a reflection of a globalised world and the rise of Asia. They now see their relationship with China as very strategic, and very long term.'[57]

The bulk of Saudi Arabia's exports to China are still supplied by its state-owned oil company, Aramco, to the China Petroleum and Chemical Corporation (Sinopec), which remains China's largest importer of foreign oil due to its much greater refining capacity than other Chinese companies.[58] Since 2001, 30,000 of the imported barrels from Saudi Arabia have been in part exchanged for Aramco being allowed to operate 600 petrol stations in China's Fujian province.[59] In 2006, following the signing of five new energy cooperation agreements,[60] including a fresh memorandum of understanding between Aramco and Sinopec,[61] the total Sino-Saudi oil trade reached $15 billion and had witnessed 40 per cent growth year-on-year since 1999. By the end of 2010, Saudi oil exports to China will increase to 1.4 million barrels per day, more than 80 per cent of which will be supplied to Sinopec.[62] Without any hint of exaggeration, this has been described by Aramco's chief executive officer, Khalid Al-Falih, as 'one of the most important energy relationships in the world.'[63] In late 2009, Al-Falih also sought to assure China that their supply of Aramco's oil was guaranteed by stating to the Xinhua News Agency 'I can tell you that China has always been given the highest consideration by Aramco to make sure that they [the Chinese customers] receive as much of their requirements as possible...'[64]

Again in second place with its hydrocarbon exports has been the UAE's Abu Dhabi, with annual oil exports to China having risen from $3.5 billion to $4.5 billion over the past five years.[65] Oman, courtesy of its aforementioned twenty-five-year history of oil exports to China,[66] still remains a significant supplier, with its oil trade with Sinopec having risen from $1.5 billion in 2002 to $4.4 billion in recent years,[67] and with gas having been traded between the two countries since 1997.[68] This has led to China overtaking Japan as Oman's primary hydrocarbon customer. Omani oil exports to China are expected to increase at a greater rate than those from other Persian Gulf suppliers, given the suitability of Omani crude oil to China's existing refining technology.[69] Because of its longer history of trading oil with China, Oman's hydrocarbon exports to China are not arranged at a government-to-government level, but are rather left to the individual state-backed companies in China to arrange.[70] At present the system still seems to be working, so for the time being the decision makers have left the arrangement alone.

Kuwait, Qatar, and Bahrain's hydrocarbon trade with China has been far more modest, but again the trajectory is still impressive, with Kuwait's supply of 200,000 barrels per day to China—currently worth $700 million—likely to double in the next few years. And although Qatar is not a major oil exporter, it was reckoned that in 2008 and 2009 almost all of its oil exports were sold to China.[71] More significantly, Qatar's gas exports to China have risen in value from almost nothing in 1995 when the first export deal was struck,[72] to just under $100 million in 1999, and to nearly $1 billion today.[73] This trajectory is likely to accelerate following the establishment of a China National Offshore Oil Corporation (CNOOC) office in Doha in mid-2009 and CNOOC's joint commitment with Petrochina to import five million tonnes of Qatargas gas from 2010 to 2035 (three million of which will be purchased by Petrochina while 2 million will be purchased by CNOOC). When commenting on the new agreement, the president of CNOOC, Fu Chengyu, acknowledged the magnitude of these gas imports, noting that 'Qatar is now a very important player in the world energy industry. Qatar and China have great complementarities in energy cooperation. China can guarantee long-term market reliability for Qatar, while Qatar can be a stable supplier for Chinese markets.'[74] In late 2009, Qatargas also set up a representative office in Beijing with the aim of marketing Qatari gas to additional Chinese companies, and it is now thought that total Qatari gas exports to China will exceed seven million tonnes by the end of 2010.[75] As the emirate seeks to double its overall gas exports to 77 million tonnes by the end of 2010 with massive expansion of its gas cooling trains in Ras Laffan Industrial City close to the North Field,[76] China is increasingly viewed as the perfect trade partner, given its continually rising demand and its willingness to enter into long term, uncomplicated contracts.[77]

This latest increase in gas exports to China does, however, appeared to have come with some political costs for Qatar, as it transpires that some of the additional exports to China in 2009 were diverted from pre-arranged sales to the US, where demand for gas had collapsed due to recession. Indeed, in October 2009 Qatar's deputy prime minister and minister for energy and industry, Abdullah bin Hamad Al-Attiyah, had already stated that 'in the coming years China will be one of the world's biggest natural gas consumers and its consumption is growing very fast…Qatar has already diverted some supplies from the US market where prices have collapsed to Chinese customers.'[78] It was then reported by the end of the month that Qatar was indeed diverting more than ten per cent of its US exports to China, as the latter was prepared to pay a premium for its Qatari supplies. When defending the move, Al-Attiyah stated that 'we have a right to divert cargoes when we can sell the gas into a better market.' The ruler of Qatar's spokesman then confirmed this stance by explaining that 'we will not go to a low price market if there is a lot of demand for our gas elsewhere...we will go to the US market only if prices justify it, but I don't think we will dump any supplies there.'[79] Interestingly, most of the diverted gas supplies are produced by RasGas—a joint venture with Exxon Mobil that shares the Ras Laffan Industrial City with Qatargas—the above-mentioned expansion of which was originally conceived when the US and western Europe were still predicted to be its primary target markets.[80]

For South Korea, the import pattern is much the same as with its larger neighbours, although, much like Japan, it requires both substantial oil and gas imports from the Persian Gulf monarchies, given its lack of domestic oil and gas reserves. Saudi Arabia has always been its greatest hydrocarbon trade partner, and has recently been supplying about 770,000 barrels of oil per day, as part of an annual oil and gas trade worth over $21 billion. However, the UAE is its second greatest trade partner, supplying about 430,000 barrels of oil per day, as part of an annual hydrocarbon trade worth $13 billion,[81] and it is likely that in the next few years the UAE will overtake Saudi Arabia to be South Korea's primary supplier, especially in light of several key non-hydrocarbon linkages between the two countries, as discussed later in this book.[82] Indeed, South Korea is already the second greatest importer of Abu Dhabi's oil after Japan.[83] Kuwait's total oil and gas exports to South Korea are also sizeable—worth $8.1 billion, while Qatar's are worth $7 billion—almost exclusively gas exports, with Oman's being worth $5.1 billion and Bahrain's being worth $300 million.[84]

4

THE NON-HYDROCARBON TRADE

The non-hydrocarbon trade that takes place between the Persian Gulf monarchies and the Pacific Asian economies is on a much smaller scale than the massive oil and gas exports and imports. Nonetheless, as demonstrated there has been an historical precedent for the importing of certain goods from Pacific Asia into the Persian Gulf, especially textiles and electrical goods. And as the latter region's per capita wealth and purchasing power accelerated dramatically with the onset of the first oil booms, the demand for such imports has continued to increase correspondingly, along with new demands for automobiles, machinery, building materials, and the many other products associated with the region's oil and construction industries. Indeed, some of the Pacific Asian cities, such as China's Yiwu—which is home to the world's largest wholesale market—are now reportedly attracting hundreds of thousands of Arab merchants annually. Although many of these will be from other Arab states, a good number will also be visiting from the Persian Gulf. In such trade hubs, which have been described by some commentators as the nodes of the new Silk Road, hundreds of Arabic translators are available and, as will be discussed later in this book, it is now much easier than before for Gulf nationals to acquire the necessary visit or employment visas for such trips.[1]

In total, the Persian Gulf monarchies' imports from Japan, China, and South Korea could now be worth as much as $63 billion per year,[2] as the latter have all sought to counter their described energy import burdens by exporting their manufactured goods and services to the very suppliers of their energy needs.[3] Importantly, there is no longer as much of an imbalance in the non-hydrocarbon trade between the two regions as there used to be, as some of the export-oriented industries that have been established in the Persian Gulf—mostly those that have been a part of government plans to diversify oil-dependent economies[4]—are now among the world's leading producers of metals, plastics, and petrochemicals. For the most part, these industries are highly competitive as they have been able to rely upon a comparative advantage of cheap and abundant energy from domestic sources.[5] Their export capacity continues to increase, and crucially most of their future surpluses are being earmarked for their Pacific Asia customers.

Table 4.1: Total non-hydrocarbon trade between the Persian Gulf and Pacific Asia, 2009 (billions of US dollars)

	Japan	China	South Korea	TOTAL
Saudi Arabia	5	1.7	3	9.7
UAE	11	30	2.9	43.9
Kuwait	2	0.3	0.7	3
Qatar	1.8	0.1	0.8	2.7
Oman	1.7	0.1	0.3	2.1
Bahrain	1.3	0.1	0.1	1.5
TOTAL	22.8	32.3	7.8	62.9

Sources: Japanese, Chinese, and South Korean Ministries for Foreign Affairs.

Since the early 1980s, Japan has been the single most important exporter to the Persian Gulf, having overtaken the United States and West Germany.[6] Japan's greatest non-hydrocarbon trade partner in the region has long been the United Arab Emirates, as a function of the aforementioned historic ties to Dubai's entrepôt re-export trade, and of the emirate's willingness to remove red tape and allow foreign companies to establish themselves and distribute their products from giant export-processing zones unencumbered by domestic legislation. Notably, these zones have released foreign companies from the need to seek local partners or sponsors.[7] Indeed, Dubai's first such export processing zone—the Jebel Ali Free Zone established in 1985—soon expanded to house over 1,500 foreign companies, of which an estimated 10 per cent were Japanese by 2001.[8] The emirate is now also home to a permanent branch of the Japanese External Trade Organization (JETRO), which offers a trade consultation service for both Japanese and Dubai businesses along with a business library and a 'business matching database' to allow

Dubai merchants to locate their most suitable Japanese counterparts.[9] Japan's trade links with the UAE have also, of course, been a function of Abu Dhabi's commitment to building up heavy, non-hydrocarbon related exports industries.[10] And also a function of the UAE's very high per capita wealth, which, as shown, is now in excess of $40,000,[11] and has led to very high per capita consumption of imported consumer durables and luxuries, including Japanese automobiles and spare parts.[12] The total non-hydrocarbon trade between the two countries is now about $6.5 billion per year, having fallen from near $11 billion in 2008 due to Japanese recession.[13] Nonetheless this still makes Japan the UAE's seventh greatest overall trade partner, and according to the Dubai Chamber of Commerce and Industry, the value of trade began to grow again by the last quarter of 2009.[14]

Japan's second greatest non-hydrocarbon trade partner in the region is Saudi Arabia, with the two countries already having begun to sign economic and technical cooperation agreements as early as 1975.[15] Presently, their non-hydrocarbon trade has mushroomed to over $5 billion—coming close to the UAE trade figure—some of which is made up of Japanese imports of Saudi metals,[16] but the vast bulk of which is made up of Saudi imports of Japanese cars, machinery, electronics, and other consumer durables. In particular, with a growing economy and with a growing youthful population, Saudi Arabia's demand for cars will continue to increase. Certainly, it is expected that annual sales of new vehicles—already at 600,000 units—will surpass 800,000 by 2013. Facilitated by special appearances at the annual Riyadh Motor Show and the Saudi Autoshop, it is likely that the majority of the new units, at least over the next few years, will be purchased from Japanese companies.[17] Nevertheless, Japanese Ministry for Foreign Affairs officials have complained that this trade is not very diversified, and have stated that Japan is taking steps to explore new trade initiatives with Saudi Arabia.[18] Among some of the more innovative recent linkages has been the exporting of Japanese water-related technologies to the western region of Saudi Arabia, following the Japan Cooperation Centre for the Middle East's (JCCME) co-establishment of the Jeddah Water Desk in cooperation with the Jeddah Chamber of Commerce and Industry (JCCI) in 2005. Since then over 1,500 Saudi trainees have undertaken professional development courses in Japanese universities relating to water treatment, sewerage, and irrigation, before returning to Saudi Arabia to implement their new skills. In 2009, the JCCI enhanced its links with Japan further by setting up a more broadly defined memorandum of understanding on 'finding new means of enhancing economic and trade relations' with JETRO.[19]

Japan's non-hydrocarbon trade with Kuwait, Qatar, and Oman is more modest—presently about $2 billion, $1.8 billion, and $1.7 billion respectively, again most of which is made up of Japanese exports of cars, machinery, and consumer durables. Despite this, these figures are likely to increase over the next few years as a result of several new initiatives. In 2006, Japan and Qatar began co-hosting a Japan-Qatar Joint Economic Committee to explore possibilities for future bilateral trade accords and to address double taxation concerns and other issues. Thus far, four formal meetings have been held and these are likely to become more frequent and involve increasing numbers of delegates.[20] Most of Japan's trade with Oman is still made up of car exports, but in Tokyo this is viewed as being satisfactory, at least for the time being, as there is believed to still be considerable potential for the Omani automobile market to grow. Of the various Japanese companies seeking a share of this market, Osaka's Hino Motors has been particularly active, having entered into a collaborative agreement in 2006 with Oman's Saud Bahwan Group to distribute their commercial and heavy construction vehicles. In late 2009, the president of Hino Motors even visited Oman to congratulate the Saud Bahwan Group on making Hino such a popular brand in the country. In the near future their operation will expand even further, with plans to build a new integrated sales, spares, and service facility in Al-Azaiba, close to Muscat, and with plans to construct a large warehouse to enable distribution across the whole of Oman.[21]

Although Bahrain remains Japan's least significant trading partner in the Persian Gulf, it is noteworthy that the non-hydrocarbon trade between the two countries has increased dramatically from $700 million in 2007[22] to nearly $1.3 billion today, and is expected to increase by a further 20 per cent over the following year.[23] Part of the explanation for this rapid rise is that with few hydrocarbon exports, Bahrain has been actively, and in many ways urgently seeking new markets for its export-oriented industries. The tiny kingdom has been especially successful in selling aluminium to Japan, which, after the US, is now Bahrain's second greatest trading partner. In summer 2009, the relationship intensified when delegations from Aluminium Bahrain (ALBA) began to tour Japan in an effort to consolidate their existing business links with Japanese customers while also searching for new opportunities.[24] In parallel, a joint economic committee was set up between the Bahraini Ministry for Finance and Industry and the Japan Bank for International Cooperation (JBIC), in order to build on the prior establishment of the loosely commercial Bahrain-Japan Friendship Society that was set up in early 2009.[25]

Overall, Japanese non-hydrocarbon trade with the Persian Gulf is set to increase even further as negotiations over a free trade agreement (FTA)[26] between Japan and the six monarchies are currently taking place,[27] having commenced in 2006.[28] However, as officials at the Japanese Ministry for Foreign Affairs have confirmed, these agreements are in many ways just symbolic as trade between Japan and the Persian Gulf monarchies is already accelerating and most obstacles are usually overcome without recourse to formal agreements.[29] Indeed, many Japanese companies have successfully established branches in the region in recent years, not just in Dubai's many export-processing zones, but in all of the Gulf states. These companies, however, still represent only a very small percentage of the total number of overseas firms active in the region.[30]

As with Japan, the UAE is presently China's greatest non-hydrocarbon trade partner in the Persian Gulf, with the total trade between the two countries now estimated to be at least $30 billion, primarily made up of imports of Chinese textiles and machinery.[31] In 1985, China and the UAE's federal government signed an agreement on trade and technological cooperation and followed this up by establishing a Joint Commission of Economic, Trade, and Technical Cooperation, which has since convened four meetings.[32] And in

Chart 4.1: Share of Japanese non-hydrocarbon trade in the Persian Gulf monarchies, 2009

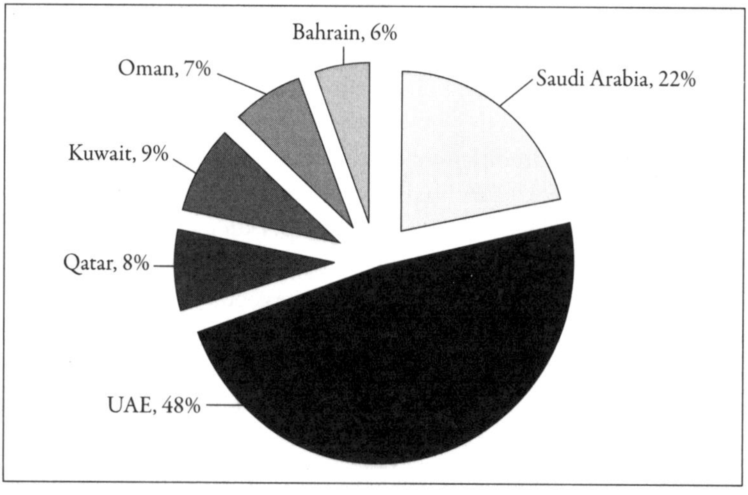

Source: Japanese Ministry for Foreign Affairs.

Chart 4.2: Japanese companies based in the Persian Gulf monarchies, 2009

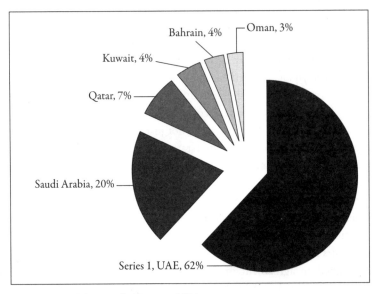

Bahrain, 4% Oman, 3%

Kuwait, 4%

Qatar, 7%

Saudi Arabia, 20%

Series 1, UAE, 62%

Source: Japanese Ministry for Foreign Affairs.

1986, China opened its first UAE centre for promoting international trade in Abu Dhabi.[33] In the near future, it is likely that China's trade with the UAE will increase massively, and will remain far ahead of Japan's non-hydrocarbon trade with the UAE. Most of this growth is expected to be as a result of Dubai's strengthening relationship with China. The emirate is already thought to be home to at least 20,000 Chinese merchants[34] and in 2008, Dubai Ports World stated that China was already Dubai's second greatest trade partner, after Iran, with Chinese non-hydrocarbon trade having increased by nearly 50 per cent since 2005.[35] In 2006, Dubai's Nakheel developers even launched ChinaMex, otherwise known as 'Dragonmart'—a massive 1.4 kilometre long, 50 hectare shopping mall in the shape of a dragon, complete with eight warehouses that specialize in the distribution and sale of Chinese goods. The project's mission statement makes clear that 'we offer Chinese traders and manufacturers a unique platform, from which they can offer their goods and services to the lucrative Middle East markets.'[36] With this and other developments, over the past two years it is likely that China has now eclipsed Iran to become the emirate's greatest trade partner. Certainly it would appear that Dubai's imports (and re-exports) from China now stand at around $19 billion, while its exports are a more modest $180 million.[37] Central to this development has been Dubai Aluminium (DUBAL), which has been the most successful of the Dubai government-backed parastatals since the onset of the global credit crunch, with its sales having risen by about 5 per cent since 2008, mostly attributed to its Chinese exports.[38] Launched in 2007, the Dubai Multi Commodities Centre (DMCC)—which is essentially a precious metals re-exporting operation that builds upon Dubai's historical expertise in gold trading and its impressive port facilities[39]—has also been enjoying a strong trade with China. Even though demand for gold in the Middle East and South Asia has fallen by 30 per cent since 2008, Chinese demand has risen by 8 per cent over the same period, making it the world's second largest consumer of gold.[40] It is also important to note that China's intensifying presence in Africa may also to lead to an increase in its re-export trade with Dubai, which, as Royal Bank of Scotland analysts have maintained, will continue to serve as China's key distribution hub for the broader region. Indeed, in 2009, Chinese trade with Africa rose 45 per cent to reach $107 billion and, significantly, much of this was with North African states, thus making Dubai a more proximate entrepôt than rival ports such as distant South Africa's Cape Town.[41]

Elsewhere in the UAE, there are further signs of strengthening non-hydrocarbon links with China. In 2009, Abu Dhabi's Borouge petrochemicals company opened a marketing office in Shanghai,[42] and Abu Dhabi's business tourism suppliers have also been targeting China, spurred on by China's National Tourism Administration—which regulates the number of Chinese nationals leaving the country—recently agreeing to loosen the visa restrictions for those businesspeople wishing to take part in tours to Abu Dhabi. Since September 2009, it is thought that the number of such tour groups visiting the emirate has already doubled, and it is expected that Abu Dhabi and eventually the rest of the UAE will begin to claim a much greater share of China's outbound business tourism market, which is currently valued at almost $15 billion per annum and set to grow by 15 per cent annually. Indeed, as Mubarak Al-Muhairi, the director general of the Abu Dhabi Tourism Authority (ADTA) has explained 'China is one of today's most important business tourism markets and it is therefore crucial that Abu Dhabi is well represented there...We cannot let this market go unnoticed. We now have the right infrastructure, destination safety and the service quality that China always requires—but we have to go out and meet it.' To this end, in 2010 ADTA, together with the Abu Dhabi National Exhibition Centre, will begin staging a series of 'destination workshops' with dozens of travel agents in Shanghai.[43]

Also of note has been Sharjah—the UAE's third most populous and third wealthiest emirate—which revealed in late 2009 that China had become its third largest trading partner, after the Sharjah Chamber of Commerce and Industry reported on a dramatic rise in Chinese imports and exports in recent years. Total Sharjah imports (mainly machinery for its new basic manufacturing industries) from China were thought to be just over $1 billion in 2009, having increased almost threefold from $369 million in 2007, while its exports were $60 million in 2009, having increased from $45 million in 2007.[44]

China's second greatest non-hydrocarbon trade partner in the Persian Gulf has for many years been Saudi Arabia, with a memorandum of understanding on bilateral trade having been signed in 1988 which, as described, was two years before China even granted diplomatic recognition to Saudi Arabia.[45] In 1992, a bilateral trade conference was staged and the following year a high level delegation from the China Council for the Promotion of International Trade visited Saudi Arabia to sign a trade and economic cooperation agreement, which conferred the status of preferential trade partner on each country.[46] In 1996, under the auspices of a Gulf Cooperation Council-China consultative mechanism, annual trade meetings began between China and Saudi Arabia, having been held alternately in Riyadh and Beijing.[47] Significantly, in 1994 the National Shipping Company of Saudi Arabia (NSCSA) began a service to Shanghai, and the following year launched a second service to Tianjin, thus making the NSCSA the first Arab shipping company to provide a permanent link to China.[48] Today, it is estimated that the total non-hydrocarbon trade between the two countries is worth $1.7 billion, mostly made up of Saudi imports of Chinese textiles and machinery,[49] thereby making Saudi Arabia China's tenth greatest international export destination.[50] Although Saudi Arabia does not yet export many products to China, this is likely to change in the near future, especially in the field of petrochemicals, where China has already become Saudi Arabia's biggest market. Indeed, Saudi Arabian Basic Industries (SABIC) has now established marketing offices in China, and over half of its 2,000–strong Asia-based workforce is presently in China. SABIC is already looking ahead to the next step, with the clear intention of setting up downstream operations in China. As its chief executive officer explained in 2006, 'China is a region where SABIC not only wants to supply products, but is also a region that it regards as strategically important for the future manufacturing of its products.'[51]

China's non-hydrocarbon trade with the other Persian Gulf monarchies is also growing, with annual trades with Kuwait, Oman, Bahrain, and Qatar being worth $260 million, $60 million, $60 million, and $50 million respectively. As with Saudi Arabia and the UAE's Abu Dhabi, China is already Kuwait's biggest market for the export of petrochemicals.[52] These relationships have all been facilitated by several initiatives and agreements similar to those made by China with Saudi Arabia and the UAE, including an agreement on economic and technical cooperation between China and Kuwait in 1989 and the setting up of a bilateral trade commission between China and Oman in 1989—which has since held five meetings. In 1990, there was also the signing of a Sino-Bahrain agreement on trade cooperation and the staging of a Chinese export commodity exhibition in Manama,[53] and in 2000, a bilateral trade commission was established between China and Qatar.[54]

As with Japan, China intends to increase its non-hydrocarbon trade with the Persian Gulf even further by reaching an FTA with all six of the monarchies in the near future. These FTA negotiations began in 2004 following a visit by a GCC delegation to China[55] that comprised of all six GCC finance ministers plus their advisors.[56] Simultaneously, a China-Arab Cooperation Forum was set up between the Chinese Ministry for Commerce and the Arab League. At the meetings of this forum, the Chinese Ministry for Commerce predicted that total trade with the Persian Gulf monarchies would reach $100 billion by 2010, not all of which would be hydrocarbon trade. Subsequent FTA negotiations were held in 2005 and 2006, by which stage agreements had been reached on tariff reductions. Although the talks have since stalled due to China's unwillingness to lift certain import restrictions on a number of non-hydrocarbon goods from the Persian Gulf, in early 2009, the concept of an FTA was reinvigorated by the president of China, who stated that 'the Gulf FTA is in the fundamental and long-term interests of both sides and will help deepen their mutually beneficial cooperation and achieve common development.' He also pledged that 'China will work actively towards signing the FTA at the earliest date.' In summer 2009, the GCC reciprocated China's sentiments by publishing a white paper entitled, *Economic relations between GCC member states and the People's Republic of China*, which similarly urged the FTA negotiations to reach a swift conclusion.[57]

Significantly, if the FTA is completed soon this will make the GCC the first organisation—ahead of even the Association of Southeast Asian Nations (ASEAN)—to conclude successfully an FTA with China. In March 2010, there were positive signs that the FTA remained on track following the launch of the first GCC-China Business Forum in Bahrain. More than 350 GCC and Chinese delegates attended the two day event in Manama, which had

Chart 4.3: Share of Chinese non-hydrocarbon trade in the
Persian Gulf monarchies, 2009

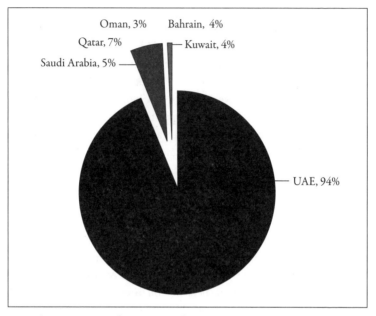

Source: Chinese Ministry for Foreign Affairs.

been jointly organised by the Federation of GCC Chambers of Commerce
and Industry and the China Council for the Promotion of International
Trade. Among the observations shared by Gulf national participants with the
local media was that 'China is a long-term partner...and there needs to be the
organisation of similar conferences where businessmen from both sides can
network with each other and build a better understanding of how to cooperate.' While others explained that 'China has only opened up in recent years...
it was not a market-driven economy before...there was this paradigm shift and
the results are for all to see,' and others urged that 'our businessmen need to
visit China frequently to see for themselves what is suitable for our market
and to see whether the products they intend to import are meeting our
standards...'[58]

South Korea's non-hydrocarbon trade with the Persian Gulf monarchies is
more modest than its neighbours, although as with Japan and China, its relationship is undoubtedly strengthening, with the Gulf states having become
collectively South Korea's second greatest export destination after China.[59]

Beginning in the 1980s, following the described inaugural visit of a South Korean president to the region[60] and the subsequent signing of twenty-six industrial partnerships between South Korean and Saudi Arabian companies, the former had begun to supply a large quantity of technical equipment to the Persian Gulf monarchies. In particular, Hyundai Corporation won a $700 million contract in 1982 to supply the parts required by plants at Saudi Arabia's Zuluf offshore oilfield, while the following year Daewoo Corporation won a $110 million contract to supply gas compression platforms to Saudi Arabia.[61] It has also been claimed that South Korean equipment was often supplied to the Persian Gulf monarchies in exchange for hydrocarbon delivery contracts, thus allowing a barter system to develop based on 'closed' trade agreements, guaranteed energy supplies, and money-free transactions.[62] The latter being particularly advantageous as it led to substantial foreign currency savings for all parties.[63] In recent years, most of the trade has been made up of cars, rubber parts, and textiles, but now South Korean exports to the Persian Gulf are considered to be much more diverse that those from Japan or China. Indeed, it is thought that cars currently make up only 20 per cent of South Korea's Gulf exports, while mobile phones, computer parts, and other consumer electrical items have recently become much bigger exports.[64] Certainly all of the biggest South Korean electronics manufacturers, including Samsung and LG, have

Chart 4.4: Share of South Korean non-hydrocarbon trade with the Persian Gulf monarchies, 2009

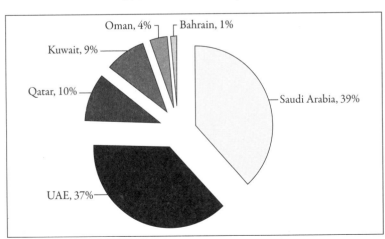

Source: South Korean Ministry for Foreign Affairs.

already established large distribution centres and marketing offices in most of the Gulf states.[65] In the UAE alone, there are presently over fifty registered South Korean companies.[66] Individually, South Korea's non-hydrocarbon trade with Saudi Arabia is about $3 billion, with the UAE $2.9 billion (up from $1.7 billion in 2005),[67] with Qatar $800 million, with Kuwait $700 million, with Oman $300 million, and with Bahrain $100 million. South Korea has not yet advanced as far as Japan and China with a GCC-wide FTA, however, negotiations did begin in summer 2008, with a second round having been held in spring 2009. Thus far, a range of tariff-related incentives have been discussed and the South Korean minister for commerce has predicted that the FTA will be finalised by the end of 2010.[68]

5

INVESTMENTS AND JOINT VENTURES

Parallel to their booming hydrocarbon and non-hydrocarbon trades, the relationship between the Persian Gulf monarchies and the Pacific Asian economies is being greatly enhanced by a substantial flow of investments between the two groups. Significantly, these investments are being made in both directions and at the highest levels, and they are predominantly being administered by massive sovereign wealth funds. Although the majority of the investments are still associated with the oil and gas industries, and—as this book will suggest—many have clear political goals in addition to their stated economic objectives, there is nonetheless strong evidence that an increasingly diverse range of non-hydrocarbon joint ventures are also being established. The only disappointment thus far, perhaps, is that few of the investments are being made by private companies. For the most part, this is due to a lack of Pacific Asian expertise on the staff of most private companies in the Persian Gulf—but this is a situation which will certainly change in the near future.[1]

In the short term, these opportunities are providing the Persian Gulf monarchies with a realistic and more hospitable alternative to the more mature Western economies for their overseas investments. Such an alternative was viewed as being particularly necessary following the September 11 attacks on New York's World Trade Center, after which many Western governments and companies did little to disguise their distrust of Gulf sovereign wealth funds, with many commentators arguing that investments from any Gulf states were not merely commercial and that power politics could be involved.[2] In early 2006, with strong opposition within the United States Congress to Dubai Ports World's attempted takeover of several US ports, there was again a

45

reminder that the Western economies were no longer the most cordial invest-ment environment.[3] In the long term, therefore, the new investment opportu-nities in Pacific Asia and the Persian Gulf will allow the economies of both regions to develop even tighter economic dependence, thus bringing the world's greatest hydrocarbon customers and suppliers even closer together.[4]

Given its slightly longer history of economic relations with the Persian Gulf monarchies, Japan is still the most active Pacific Asian investor in the region. In recent years, Japan's investments in the Persian Gulf have continued to mushroom, with annual investments in Saudi Arabia alone having increased from $9.3 billion in 2003 to $31.6 billion in 2007—a 340 per cent increase in four years.[5] Today, unsurprisingly, Japan is by far the largest foreign investor in Saudi Arabia, with billions of dollars worth of active investments currently being distributed among twenty-four different projects, including sixteen industrial projects and eight service sector projects.[6] Specifically, Japan's Sumi-tomo Chemical Company has partnered with Saudi Arabia's Aramco on the Rabigh project—a petrochemical complex in Saudi Arabia that will cost $10 billion to build.[7] And in summer 2009, the two countries entered into a $1 bil-lion joint venture when the Saudi Basic Industries Corporation and Japan's Mitsubishi Rayon agreed to build an acrylics factory in Saudi Arabia, with Mitsubishi holding the majority stake.[8] As discussed, Japan has been heavily involved in selling water-related technologies to Saudi Arabia, and recently it has begun to make water-related investments in the kingdom. It has already financed several water projects at Musk Lake in Jeddah and it now seems that further such joint ventures are being planned. In late 2009, several Japanese experts in water supply technology were invited to the Jeddah Chamber for Commerce and Industry to hold talks with Saudi businessmen and water tech-nology investors. The JCCI secretary general, Mustafa Kamal Sabri noted the 'huge mutual effort between Saudi Arabia and Japan in such investments'. He also explained that a follow-up meeting would be held in Tokyo, with the aim of establishing a permanent Japanese Water Office in the Persian Gulf, with Jeddah as its headquarters. Significantly, the head of the Japanese delegation insisted that 'by Saudi Arabia using the latest Japanese technologies with regard to the desalination of seawater the water crisis in Jeddah could be solved one day.'[9] Although examples of investments in the other direction are presently much thinner, it is nonetheless likely that Saudi companies will also begin to seek opportunities in Japan. Indeed, since 2004, has held a 15 per cent stake in Japan's fifth largest oil company, Showa Shell Sekiyu.[10] Even though this transfer was the result of Showa's Anglo-Dutch partner, Royal Dutch Shell,

Chart 5.1: Japanese annual investments in Saudi Arabia and the UAE
(billions of US dollars)

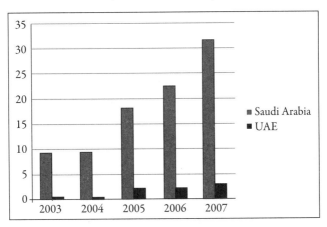

Source: Japanese Ministry for Finance.

choosing to sell directly to Aramco, it is likely that the sale will serve as a precedent for other Saudi companies with an interest in investing in Japan's hydrocarbon companies.[11]

Although Japan's investments in the United Arab Emirates have been more modest than in Saudi Arabia, the trajectory of their increase is if anything even more impressive, with annual investments having increased from $600 million in 2003 to $3.1 billion in 2007—a six–fold increase.[12] Notably, Abu Dhabi's third largest sovereign wealth fund, the International Petroleum Investment Company (IPIC), has recently sought a $5 billion injection from Japan's Mitsubishi UFJ Financial Group and the Sumitomo Mitsui Banking Corporation. This package will, in turn, allow these Japanese banks to have an interest in some of IPIC's overseas investments, including its purchase of Canada's Nova Chemicals Corporation and its recently acquired stake in Spain's Compañia Española de Petroleos (CEPSA).[13] In the other direction Japan is strongly committed to seeking foreign direct investment from the UAE. In 2007, Dubai International Capital (DIC)—the international investment arm of Dubai Holdings, an umbrella organisation owned by the ruler of Dubai—purchased a 'substantial stake' in the beleaguered Sony Corporation, making this the first ever major UAE investment in Japan.[14] And in summer 2009, the Japan External Trade Organisation, the aforementioned government-backed entity tasked with matching up foreign companies with

Japanese companies, named the UAE as one of its top three target countries for sourcing foreign direct investment, along with Russia and Brazil. Since its announcement, JETRO has followed up by holding several FDI-related seminars in Abu Dhabi with the emirate's various sovereign wealth funds including the Mubadala Development Corporation, the Abu Dhabi Investment Authority (ADIA), and the Abu Dhabi Investment Corporation, as well as IPIC. Since JETRO's drive began, IPIC has taken a 21 per cent, $780 million stake in Japan's Cosmo Oil Company[15] which, as described, has recently had its major Abu Dhabi offshore oil concession renewed ahead of schedule,[16] thus strengthening further the Japanese-UAE interdependence on several levels. Other notable Japanese interests in the Persian Gulf monarchies currently include over $5 billion of investments in five hydrocarbon and infrastructural projects in Qatar, and a total of $260 million of investments in five infrastructural projects in Oman.[17] Although Japan's investment relationship with Kuwait still remains in its infancy, this too is likely to strengthen, with the Kuwait Investment Authority (KIA) having stated in 2008 that it intends to increase by threefold its investments in Japan.[18]

In early 2005, the Chinese Ministry for Commerce revealed that Chinese investments in the Persian Gulf monarchies had already reached $5 billion, while Persian Gulf investments in China totaled $700 million.[19] With a significant number of further investments and joint ventures since that announcement, these figures have since mushroomed, and it is predicted that China's interests will soon even overtake Japan's in the region. In particular, state-backed Chinese companies have been seeking investments that will help to build up their oil refining industries, while almost all of the Gulf States have been seeking to secure a dominant presence in the fast growing industries of what they believe to be the new Asian economic superpower.[20]

At present, China's greatest investment partner in the Persian Gulf is Kuwait. In the 1980s, the Kuwait Pacific Finance Company was established to facilitate money flows between the two countries while in parallel the Hong Kong Metropolitan Bank and the UBAN International—both established during the latter years of Britain's Hong Kong protectorate—were similarly specialising in China-Kuwait investments.[21] In 1984, a subsidiary of the Kuwait Petroleum Company (KPC) took a 15 per cent stake in China's Yacheng offshore gasfield, while the following year KPC set up a joint venture—the Sino Arab Chemical Fertilizer Company (SACF) to invest in the Qilu petrochemicals facility in China's eastern Shandong province.[22] KPC held 60 per cent of SACF's capital, with the other 40 per cent being held by the Chinese National Chemical Construction Company.[23] Later in 1985, the two countries signed an investment guarantee to provide increased protection for joint China-Kuwait joint investments.[24] Since 2005, KIA alone has increased its portfolio share in the Pacific Asian economies (most of it in Chinese investments) from 10 to 20 per cent,[25] and it is now the largest foreign investor in the Industrial and Commercial Bank of China,[26] having purchased $700 million worth of shares in 2006. This has effectively made the Kuwaiti government the biggest investor in one of China's first major public offerings. The relationship between the two countries was also strengthened greatly following the setting up of a $9 billion joint venture between KPC and Sinopec in 2005. Since then, the two companies have been jointly financing the construction of a massive 300,000 barrels per day capacity oil refinery and ethylene plant in China's southern Guangdong province. Although the exact location of these facilities has since been changed due to environmental concerns raised by nearby Hong Kong,[27] the project is still expected to come online in 2013 and will become China's largest ever joint project.[28]

In the other direction, China may soon become heavily involved in Kuwaiti projects, with Sinopec currently having a sizeable stake in an international consortium that is bidding for an $8 billion infrastructural programme.[29] But the most innovative and symbolic aspect of the investments between the two countries has been the establishment of the Kuwait-China Investment Company (KCIC) in 2005. Set up by the Kuwait government, the KCIC is 15 per cent owned by KIA and it now has a capital base of about $350 million, about half of which is held in cash in order to facilitate rapid responses to strategic opportunities. It has specialised in investments in Chinese agribusinesses; particularly those producing crops with a high export value such as rice, wheat, corn, and sorghum. Significantly, KCIC's investments in China have been defended as being purely commercial and not primarily connected to Kuwait's or the region's looming food security problem—unlike the recent deals between the UAE and other Persian Gulf monarchies with Pakistan and Kazakhstan, which clearly are evidence of such a concern.[30] In 2009, the managing director of KCIC stated simply that: 'we think it is an opportune sector that will help Pacific-Asia effectively become the bread basket of the world...we think food security, in the long term, is better served by collaborative investment in Asia as opposed to securing crops exclusively for one country.' He also stated of KCIC's existing collaborations with Chinese agribusinesses that: 'our financial skills are paired with agri-sector skills and hopefully both of these skills can help mitigate some of the risks and provide a decent return for the investors.'[31]

Beyond Kuwait, China is also heavily involved with Saudi Arabia, with Aramco having led the way, as it has done with Japanese investments. Tellingly, the company now has more offices in China than in any other country,[32] and it has also taken a 25 per cent stake in a major joint venture with Sinopec and the China National Petroleum Corporation's (CNPC) Petrochina subsidiary in 2001.[33] The venture, named the Fujian Refining and Petrochemical Company (FREP) has involved the two companies expanding an existing refinery in China's southeastern Fujian province along with building a brand new ethylene plant. In November 2009, the Fujian refinery went into operation, thereby increasing the province's annual refining capacity from four million to twelve million tonnes. Moreover, Aramco is now the largest shareholder in the Thalin refinery project in China, and in the near future, it may embark on another joint venture with two Chinese companies to build a refinery in the Chinese coastal city of Qingdao, again with Aramco taking the majority stake.[34] This could lead to the building of one of the largest oil refining facilities in the world and may require as much as $6 billion to complete. Aramco's chief executive officer, Khalid Al-Falih, appears positive but cautious on such ambitious future developments, having stated that talks are going ahead but that 'we want to operate our existing [Fujian] joint venture for a little while longer to see if it will be profitable and make money before we move further to new investments... for any project we build, there is a period to create enough profit...then we can consider further expansion and investment.'[35] Similarly to Aramco, SABIC has already helped to initiate three petrochemicals projects in China as part of its 'China Plan', which aims to facilitate mutual investments between the two countries by supporting China's economic development and, as its premier supplier of petrochemicals, helping to satisfy its ever-increasing demand.[36] And in 2009, SABIC entered into an agreement to build a fourth petrochemical complex, costing $3 billion, in China's northeastern Tianjin province.[37]

In the other direction, Sinopec has recently embarked on yet another joint venture with Aramco, taking an 80 per cent, $300 million, stake in a new oil and gas exploration company in Saudi Arabia.[38] Some commentators believe that this particular partnership is more symbolic than practical as Sinopec has far less experience of developing gasfields than Aramco. Indeed, Aramco may see the agreement as primarily an effort to strengthen even further its already privileged position in investing in China's booming refining industry.[39] Other examples of Chinese investments in Saudi Arabia include some financing of the building of telecommunications infrastructure in various parts of the kingdom[40] in addition to a Chinese aluminum company's investment in a phosphate plant in northern Saudi Arabia. The beginning of construction on a second Saudi-Chinese phosphate plant in the new Jazan Economic City[41] is also of great significance, as this complex, when complete, is likely to become one of the busiest ports in the Middle East. Close to the mouth of the Red Sea, it will allow all companies that have a presence in the development to have very good access to shipping routes between Europe, Asia, and East Africa, while also being well placed to receive raw materials from surrounding countries that are not presently well equipped with manufacturing and processing facilities.

Elsewhere in the Persian Gulf, the Qatari Investment Authority (QIA) has recently followed Kuwait's lead and has signaled its intent to purchase $200 million worth of shares in subsequent public offerings from the Industrial and Commercial Bank of China.[42] It has also opened a permanent office in China with the intention of pursuing further sovereign wealth investment opportunities in the country, with QIA's CEO, Ahmad Al-Sayed, having explained that 'China and Asia are growth markets for Qatar—we are really serious about finding the right opportunities there.'[43] Most significantly perhaps, in summer 2009, it was announced that Qatar Petroleum would enter into a joint venture with Petrochina worth $12 billion. This deal, if followed through, would eclipse even Kuwait's investments in China and would lead to the construction of a new petrochemicals plant in China's eastern Zhejiang province, along with an oil refinery, an ethylene plant, and a port for oil supertankers.[44] In the other direction, in 2008, China chose Qatar as the location to open its first bank in the Middle East. Launched just one month after the collapse of Lehman Brothers in the US, the president of the Industrial and Commercial Bank of China defended his move into the Persian Gulf by stating that his bank—presumably in contrast to the existing multinationals in the region—'will enjoy the advantages of starting in the region with a clean slate... we are just a newcomer... we don't have any burden. Last year so many local banks and even Western banks, they lacked money, and were even maybe in crisis, so we found many opportunities.' He also explained the late arrival of Chinese banks in the region on the grounds that 'it takes time to understand each other.' Over the course of 2009, the Industrial and Commercial Bank of China's Qatar branch grew steadily with its loan book reaching $500 million, resulting in net profits of approximately $3 million. Thus far, most of its business has been in offering commercial banking services to Chinese companies already in the Persian Gulf, in addition to working with Gulf companies that have entered into joint ventures with Chinese companies, and also a select number of large Qatari clients including Qatar Airways and Qatar Telecommunications. In 2010, the bank expects to double its profits, offer investment banking services in the region, and expand into Saudi Arabia and the UAE—where it already provides services for Abu Dhabi's Mubadala Development Corporation and IPIC.[45] In the near future, Qatar is also likely to be one of the first subscribers to South Korea's new Islamic *sukuk* bonds, which are being developed specifically with investors from the Persian Gulf monarchies in mind. In late 2009, a revision was proposed to South Korea's tax laws by the vice minister for strategy and finance. Following the revision's approval, he announced that South Korea would launch its first sukuk in early 2010, which would be based on investments in twenty-four large state-backed corporations and 130 smaller privately owned companies. He suggested that Qatari investors would be among those initially sought to buy into the sukuk.[46]

Much like its neighbours, the UAE, and more specifically Dubai, is also investing in China, and has been since the late 1980s following the establishment of the Dubai Oriental Finance Company.[47] In 1988 the UAE's Al-Otaiba Group invested $360 million in an oil refinery project in the Shenzen special economic zone in China's Guangdong province. Reportedly this was the largest foreign investment in China that year.[48] More recently the aforementioned government-owned Dubai Ports World—a subsidiary of the Dubai World parastatal—has made significant investments in China, and now operates seven container terminals in the country, three of them in Hong Kong, with none of the opposition the company experienced in its earlier bid to operate ports in the US. Crucially, Dubai Ports World's success has been attributed to its well-developed partnership with China's Tianjin Port Group Company.[49] And in the near future, the joint venture will also open a terminal in China's northeastern Qingdao province. The company now also operates a terminal in South Korea, and in other parts of East Asia, it has begun to open terminals in Indonesia, Thailand, and the Philippines.[50] In 2009, it announced that it would also take an 80 per cent stake in a joint venture with both a Chinese company and Vietnam's state-owned Tan Thuan Industrial Promotion Company in order to build yet another Asian container port—the Saigon Premier Container Terminal—outside of Ho Chi Minh City.[51]

Other Dubai investments in China may be managed by the new China Dubai Capital—a fund jointly established in 2008 by DIC and China's First Eastern Investment Group—the leading Chinese private equity firm. Together, the companies hope to identify quality investments in China for Dubai-based companies and investors,[52] and it is thought that the fund had attracted $500 million in investments shortly after opening, and had closed by the end of 2008 with nearly $1 billion in investments. Commenting on this apparent success the CEO of DIC at the time stated that 'we are pleased to partner with First Eastern...it has an unrivalled track record in direct investments in China. Through this fund, we will invest in feasible and profitable business opportunities in commercially attractive sectors. The establishment of China Dubai Capital provides investors with the opportunity to participate in a vehicle which will generate superior returns.' Similarly, the CEO of First Eastern Investment Group noted that 'this is a unique opportunity to create a win-win situation for China and the UAE. Chinese companies are very attracted by the opportunities arising from the opening up of the Gulf region. The UAE, particularly Dubai, is strategically positioned as the natural gateway for GCC access, as well as for capital-raising through its established securities markets. Our new fund will be in a great position to generate exciting returns from the synergies between these two regions.'[53] Significantly, since these statements First Eastern Investment Group has become the first Chinese financial company to open a branch in the Dubai International Finance Centre (DIFC)—a free zone for international financial companies—and it is expected that it will soon be launching a similar fund to China Dubai Capital but with a Saudi Arabian partner.[54]

It is also important to note that while Dubai's real estate sector was still booming, several of the Emirate's developers had also intended to branch out into international real estate opportunities, and China was viewed as one of the best opportunities for such investment. While these investments are now unlikely to take place given the severe Dubai crash discussed later in this book,[55] the actors involved and the scale of the proposed projects are nonetheless worth considering. Emaar International, a division of Emaar Properties—Dubai's first and biggest real estate developer—had already set up an office in Shanghai in summer 2006 and had begun to hold negotiations with potential Chinese partners. Its plans were thought to include various high-end residential and commercial real estate ventures, in addition to luxury hotels and even some hospitals. Notably, in summer 2008, Emaar International signed a memorandum of understanding with Shanghai's China-News Enterprise Development Limited—a government owned company—to explore such possibilities. Although Emaar International stated in October 2009 that it was still considering such developments in China, it does not appear that the projects have moved forward, seemingly due to Dubai's domestic problems and the increasing necessity for retrenchment in the emirate.[56] Similarly bullish before the crash, Dubai's Damac Properties had also signaled their intention to invest in China, beginning with a proposed $2.7 billion residential and commercial project in the Tanggu district, while the Jumeirah Group—another component of Dubai Holdings—announced it would develop a hotel in Shanghai.[57] Most ambitious, or perhaps absurd, of the Dubai-China proposals was the plan of Dubai's Meydan developer to enter into a $4 billion joint venture with two Chinese companies to build a giant 'horse city' near to the city of Tianjin. If ever completed, the new city will comprised of equestrian facilities and residential units to accommodate over 20,000 people.[58]

In the other direction, China's Dashang Corporation was set to invest more than $200 million in Dubai's retail sector, likely financing the development of more shopping malls, but again this is likely to have been placed on hold due to the emirate's difficulties.[59] Interestingly, in early 2010 Chinese interest in Dubai seemingly began to pick up again as investors from Wenzhou—a port city in southeastern China which is renowned for its entrepreneurial spirit—began to visit the emirate in search of distressed real estate assets. Indeed, it was reported that over twenty real estate and investment firms from the city visited Dubai in January 2010, presumably in an effort to determine whether Dubai property prices—at less than 40 per cent of their 2008 peak—had bottomed out in the wake of the crash. Having already invested about $730 million in Dubai real estate during the boom years, Wenzhou investors are believed to have already suffered losses of about $150 million—including an individual $28 million investment in one of the artificial islands that makes up the 'World'—a project that is now suspended. But with Wenzhou residential properties now selling for close to $9000 per square metre due to lack of supply, Dubai real estate is still regarded as an attractive and relatively affordable investment.[60] Often overlooked, the UAE's third most populous emirate—Sharjah— has enjoyed an equal if not more impressive trajectory at attracting Chinese investment over the past two years. Without a fragile real estate sector or a significant tourism industry, Sharjah has apparently maintained investor confidence in its light manufacturing industries, with Chinese investments in the sector having grown by over 100 per cent from 2008 to 2009. Increasingly proactive, Sharjah's Economic Development Department even invited a Chinese delegation to Sharjah in late 2009 to discuss opportunities for Chinese companies to invest in Sharjah's planned technology-related industries.[61]

Although talks began in the late 1990s to establish a joint venture to build a new oil refinery in China,[62] Abu Dhabi has thus far been more cautious than Dubai with regard to investing in China. Nonetheless, there are now some good proxy examples: IPIC has a 65 per cent controlling stake in Borealis[63]—a plastics company based in Austria that has links with the Abu Dhabi Polymers Company—and in turn, Borealis is investing in a polypropylene plant in China, to help boost the supply of plastics for the latter's booming automobile industry,[64] which is now made up of more than forty-five car manufacturers, including Beijing Automobile Works and Chery Automobile.[65] With the opening of a Hong Kong branch of the National Bank of Abu Dhabi (NBAD) in late 2009, the Abu Dhabi-China link will likely strengthen much further over the next few years. Analysts have interpreted the move as being a direct response 'to rapidly growing trade flows between China and the Gulf...it will make it easier for companies investing in either direction to carry out transactions...and it's a reflection of the growing commercial clout of the relationship between China and the Gulf.'[66] The branch is currently being staffed by about thirty personnel (mostly made up of Chinese nationals) and it is intended that it will eventually fund itself entirely through its earnings. Already there are promising signs, with a Hong Kong-based consultancy company being used by the bank to identify Chinese investors for projects in Abu Dhabi, and with the bank having already been contacted by several Chinese companies specializing in infrastructure and a number of smaller firms seeking local partners for joint ventures in Abu Dhabi. Moreover, it has been announced that in the near future NBAD will open branches on mainland China, again with an emphasis on hiring local employees. This strategy has been explained on both cultural and pragmatic grounds, with NBAD's spokesman stating that 'there's a huge difference between Asian firms investing into China vis-à-vis other foreign firms. The cultural difference is key...foreign investors have certain concerns about the legal situation and protocols in China. You see all kinds of troubles—they can't find the right people, they appoint foreign managers to run manufacturing plants who then come into conflict with local representatives. But these are the challenges one faces in an emerging market.'[67]

It is also noteworthy that Abu Dhabi is increasingly involved in other East Asian opportunities, which could serve as blueprints for future Chinese or South Korean projects. Most notably, in summer 2008, its Mubadala Development Corporation acquired the Indonesia-based Pearl Energy hydrocarbon exploration and production company. This allowed Mubadala to inherit Pearl's portfolio of concessions and production assets in several East Asian countries, including three oilfields in Indonesia, the Jasmine offshore oilfield in the Gulf of Thailand, and other resources in Vietnam and the Philippines.[68] In 2008, Mubadala also took a major stake in a joint venture to develop a large residential and commercial real estate opportunity in Malaysia's Medini Iskandar Development City with the aim of 'securing long term financial and strategic returns for Abu Dhabi.' In 2009, this was followed up by Mubadala agreeing to invest $1 billion into a new Malaysian fund managed by 1 Malaysia Development Berhad (1MDB) that would specialise in investments in energy, real estate, and tourism projects in Malaysia.[69]

While the UAE does not yet have major investments or joint ventures with South Korea, this is likely to change in the near future, especially following the successful South Korean bid to construct the UAE's first nuclear power plants, as discussed later in this book.[70] Indeed, the Korea Electric Power Corporation (KEPCO)—South Korea's largest parastatal—is facing competition from the private sector, which by 2015 is likely to account for more than 10 per cent of the domestic South Korean market. As such, an increasingly outward looking KEPCO has reaffirmed its commitment to seeking foreign direct investment and collaborative opportunities with international partners, with Abu Dhabi now being the most likely candidate.[71] Another possible avenue for joint ventures is the semiconductor industry, with Abu Dhabi's Advanced Technology Investment Company (ATIC) having signed a memorandum of understanding in early 2010 with South Korea's Semiconductor Industry Association (KSIA). The former, which has already formed a joint venture company—Global Foundries—with the US, Advanced Micro Devices (AMD) as part of the emirate's long term objective of becoming a regional centre for high technology manufacturing,[72] is seemingly enthusiastic to build further partnerships. And the KSIA agreement will now allow ATIC to communicate directly with South Korea's semiconductor giants, notably Samsung and Hynix.[73] Certainly, the latter, which is now the world's second largest chip manufacturer, is already believed to have made an approach to Abu Dhabi.[74] Other investment opportunities may be identified by both countries at the various investor road shows that South Korea has begun to hold in Abu Dhabi since late 2009. These have followed a statement made by the South Korean prime minister that 'we would like to see more of the funds from Abu Dhabi come to Korea to invest. If we find really good partners in the private sector, even in the government sector, then we can make a much greater improvement in our relationship.' The first of these shows, coordinated by the South Korean Ministry for Strategy and Finance, reportedly attracted dozens of representatives from major UAE developers and sovereign wealth funds.[75] In 2010, it is expected that similar road shows will begin to take place in other Persian Gulf monarchies, most likely in Qatar and Kuwait.

6

CONSTRUCTION AND LABOUR CONTRACTS

Both state-backed and private construction and labour companies in the Pacific Asian economies have been winning contracts in the Persian Gulf monarchies for over twenty-five years. The China National Petroleum Corporation began supplying labourers for large scale infrastructure projects in Kuwait as early as 1983, and by 1989, there were over 175 labour and construction contracts in place between the two countries, with an estimated 20,000 Chinese labourers being based in Kuwait.[1] Similarly, in the 1990s, a number of South Korean companies began to pick up contracts in Saudi Arabia and Kuwait,[2] while the China Petrochemical Corporation won the contract to renovate Kuwait's damaged Al-Ahmadi refinery in 1992 as part of the emirate's post-war reconstruction.[3] Soon after, the CNPC signed a $400 million contract to build two oil storage depots in western Kuwait, and in 1996, the Chinese Maritime Engineering Company repaired another damaged Kuwaiti refinery in Shuybah.[4] Chinese companies were also contracted to participate in the construction of Fujairah's dry docks on the Indian Ocean coastline of the United Arab Emirates.[5] In total, it was estimated that Pacific Asian companies signed about $10 billion worth of construction contracts across the region in the 1990s.[6] In a few cases, especially from Saudi Arabia, Persian Gulf construction companies were sometimes even winning contracts in the Pacific Asian states. Notably, in 1993, the Al-Zamil Steel Building Company from Riyadh began construction on an air-conditioning plant in China's Shenzen special economic zone.[7] Since 2000, a number of Chinese companies have also been supplying labourers for tourism and real estate projects in the UAE, most notably the luxury hotels that have been built in Fujairah.[8]

Over the last few years, however, there has been an explosion in the number of major contracts awarded to Pacific Asian companies in the Persian Gulf monarchies. Most of these have been both to build and supply the labour for multi-billion dollar developments and, significantly, in many cases the successful Japanese, Chinese, and South Korean companies have had to compete against Arab and Western companies, most of which have enjoyed a much longer history of winning contracts in the region and have usually sourced their labour from South Asia. Undoubtedly, these new Pacific Asian contracts have served to solidify further the growing economic interdependence between the two regions while also taking advantage of the Pacific Asian companies' experience, technologies, and—in China's case—access to abundant labour. Indeed, the latter is a significant although rarely discussed advantage when it comes to winning contracts, as even if Chinese labour may come at a slightly higher cost than labour from India, Pakistan, or Bangladesh,[9] it is likely viewed as less problematic by the governments of the Persian Gulf monarchies. Certainly the presence of thousands of Chinese or other Pacific Asian labourers, few of whom are Muslim or can speak Arabic, is less likely to pose a security threat to these states as there will be fewer opportunities for their integration with the regular resident population or for radical groups to identify and communicate with recruits in the labour camps.

Notable among the recent success stories has been Japan's Shimizu Corporation, which won a high profile contract in 2006 to construct the Dubai Marina Residences real estate project in Dubai's prosperous Jumeirah district, defeating several regional competitors in the process.[10] Soon after, several other Japanese companies went on to win large contracts to construct other real estate developments and physical infrastructure in Dubai, including segments of the city's new, two-line metro system. In 2007, China's Jingye Construction Engineering Company won an equally lucrative contract in Dubai, with an opportunity to build various skyscrapers and stadia in Dubai Sports City in cooperation with the UAE-based Emirates Building Systems.[11] Since 2006, the China Construction Company has also been active in the emirate, winning the contract to build Al-Hekma Tower—a project developed by Abu Dhabi's Pearl Properties.[12] Remarkably, by the close of 2008, it was estimated that Chinese companies had secured over $2 billion in construction contracts in Dubai and elsewhere in the UAE,[13] with its Zhongon Construction Group alone having won over $100 million of real estate business in the country.[14] In 2009, it was estimated that a further $1.3 billion of contracts had been won.[15] On the labour front, it was estimated that there were about 80,000 Chinese workers based in the UAE in 2009, and some analysts have predicted that the number could increase to 200,000 in the near future.[16]

Elsewhere in the Persian Gulf, China has been similarly successful. In summer 2009, the China Railway Construction Company (CRCC) won a reportedly fierce contest to be awarded a $500 million contract by the Ministry for Education in Saudi Arabia. This will require the Chinese company to build 200 primary and secondary schools to accommodate 140,000 pupils over a period of one year. Although this will represent only a small fraction of the 3,500 schools that are now under construction in Saudi Arabia, mostly by Arab companies, this Chinese involvement nonetheless represents a significant departure for the Saudi authorities.[17] Earlier in 2009, China's Sinopec won a similarly rewarding contract in Kuwait, worth $400 million, to build five new oil and gas stations. Alone, these new Chinese-built installations will boost Kuwait's oil production by over four million barrels per day by 2020.[18]

But of the three principal Pacific Asian states, it has been South Korea that has made the greatest inroads into the Persian Gulf's construction and labour sector, despite being a relative latecomer to the region's economy, at least compared to its neighbours. In 1980, the Dong Ah Industrial Company won the commission to build Libya's giant manmade river, thus signalling South Korea's entry into the Middle East,[19] and this was soon followed by the Korean Shipbuilding and Engineering Company winning a contract in 1982 for the construction of a new ship-repair yard in the Saudi Arabian port of Jeddah, and the Hella Construction Company's winning of a $110 million contract later that year for the construction of a new Saudi Arabian export refinery in Jubail. In 1983, South Korea's Lucky Oil won a contract to build a petrochemicals complex in Jubail, while Samsung Engineering and Construction began work on a $26 million project to build eight storage tanks in Mina Al-Ahmadi. Hyundai Corporation alone was understood to have won $3.1 billion worth of construction contracts in the Persian Gulf during the 1980s, while other South Korean companies began to work on a large number of military and civilian constructions in Saudi Arabia, including the Saudi Arabia National Centre for Science and Technology, barracks and housing in the eastern province, the drilling of water wells, the building of hospitals and clinics, and the construction of roads and bridges. By the 1990s, it was estimated that over 90 per cent of South Korean construction work was originating in the Persian Gulf with South Korean companies sometimes even acquiring market shares in Persian Gulf monarchies that were in excess of South Korea's total value of oil imports from those countries.[20] One analyst claimed this was 'taking billions of dollars of the "petrodollars" away from the established Western concerns,' while others explained that 'the South Korean conglomerates seemed to have combined their technological expertise with good management sense and cheap and skilled labour, with devastating effect as far as competition from the West was concerned.'[21]

It was, however, in 2003 when Samsung Engineering and Construction began work on the Abu Dhabi Investment Authority's iconic new corniche headquarters, and in 2004 when the same company took on a similarly symbolic role with Dubai's 160 storey Burj Khalifa skyscraper (formerly known as the Burj Dubai), that South Korean companies became perhaps the premier and most visible presence in the Persian Gulf's construction industry. Much of their subsequent success has been ascribed to their low fees, flexibility, and willingness to take on some risk.[22] South Korean construction companies have also benefited from currency fluctuations, especially in 2008 and early 2009, when the rapid depreciation of the Korean *won* from 1,000 per US dollar to nearly 1,600 per US dollar gave their bidders great price competitiveness over international rivals.[23] A track record of keeping to schedules also seems significant, with one South Korean analyst explaining that 'Korean players have demonstrated a competitive edge both in constructing plants and high-rise skyscrapers. They have won the trust of Gulf nations as they have kept to deadlines unlike their Western rivals.'[24] Moreover, as discussed later in this book,[25] the South Korean government has repeatedly provided very high-level diplomatic support for construction companies in their efforts to outflank rival foreign bidders. From the perspective of Gulf governments and developers, such South Korean enthusiasm is very welcome as it is already thought to have contributed to a more vibrant and competitive sector. As one Abu Dhabi official recently admitted, South Korea is currently serving the UAE very well as it is prompting much cheaper bids from other companies.[26]

In total, it is has been estimated that South Korean companies won $22.8 billion worth of construction contracts in the Persian Gulf monarchies in 2007, and just over $27 billion in 2008. With total Gulf construction contracts in 2008 being worth $47.6 billion,[27] this means that South Korea had secured an impressive 57 per cent of the region's business. Although 2009 is not expected to have been so lucrative, given the rather harsh impact of the global credit crunch on some of the Persian Gulf monarchies, South Korean companies have nonetheless won several further multi-billion dollar contracts and, as the final chapter of this book will discuss, South Korean companies ended the year on the highest possible note with a massive Abu Dhabi contract to construct four nuclear plants.[28] Among the other UAE projects, three of the five new gas facilities in Abu Dhabi's Habshan region—to be operated by Abu Dhabi Gas Industries (GASCO)—will be constructed by South Korea's Hyundai Engineering and Construction, the GS Engineering and Construction Company, and Hyundai Heavy Industries, all of which won their contracts in 2009, totaling $4.9 billion. Specifically, Hyundai Engineering and Construction's contract is worth $1.7 billion.[29] It will last for four years and will involve building storage and wastewater facilities, in addition to power facilities. Hyundai Heavy Industries' contract is worth $1 billion and the GS Engineering and Construction Company's contract is worth $2.2 billion, and both will last for five years. The latter will build similar facilities alongside Hyundai Engineering and Construction and although it will be cooperating with Britain's Petrofac as part of a joint venture, it will hold a 55 per cent majority stake in the consortium. Remarkably, Hyundai Engineering and Construction is already believed to be working on nine other projects in the UAE.

Other current projects in the UAE include SK Engineering and Construction's contract to build the compression units at the Abu Dhabi Company for Onshore Oil Operations' (ADCO) Bab onshore gasfield. Significantly, it is thought that SK's bid, at $800 million, was over $100 million lower than the next competitor's.[30] Also in 2009, Samsung Engineering and Construction won a contract to build Borouge's new petrochemicals conversion unit in Abu Dhabi, while the GS Engineering and Construction Company won both a contract to build a 'green diesel facility' in the emirate's hinterland[31] and a $3.1 billion contract to build a new crude oil refinery at Ruwais, to the west of Abu Dhabi, by 2014.[32] Perhaps most symbolically, at the close of 2009, a consortium of three South Korean companies defeated fourteen other international bidders to win another $4.4 billion of construction work in the UAE. Collectively these contracts were awarded by the Abu Dhabi Oil Refining Company (Takreer) and will be for four years of work. Samsung Engineering and Construction was awarded the offsite and utilities package, worth $2.7 billion, Daewoo Engineering and Construction Company was awarded the tanking and piping package, worth $1.2 billion, while the GS Engineering and Construction Company was awarded the maritime facilities component, worth $500 million.[33] In early 2010, South Korean companies continued to win work in the sector, with Samsung Engineering and Construction and SK Engineering and Construction securing $2.7 billion and $2.1 billions contracts, respectively, for further work at Ruwais.[34] South Korean companies have now also become involved in the UAE's housing construction industry, with STX Construction having begun work on a large-sized residential complex in Abu Dhabi following a successful bid at $181 million. With a rapidly expanding national population, a strong distributive economy, and a long-running tradition of building houses for its nationals, this sector of Abu Dhabi's construction industry will continue to be a lucrative opportunity for such companies.[35] Soon, South Korean companies will also be bidding to build some of the iconic new cultural buildings planned for Abu Dhabi's Saadiyat Island, including its branches of the Louvre and the Guggenheim, in addition to the new Zayed National Museum.[36]

In Saudi Arabia, perhaps South Korea's second most active market, Hyundai Engineering and Construction has recently completed the construction of new gas processing facilities in at the Khurais field and in early 2009, it won a $1.9 billion contract to build further gas processing facilities in the Karan field, on behalf of Aramco. Meanwhile, three other major South Korean companies— Daelim Industrial, SK Engineering and Construction, and Samsung Engineering and Construction—have won a combined $2.8 billion contract to build a new refinery and petrochemicals plant in Saudi Arabia.[37] In Qatar, there has also been some success for South Korea, with Hyundai Engineering and Construction forming a consortium with Italy's Saipem to build a new fertilizer plant—the QAFCO-6 project—for Industries Qatar. This three year contract is worth $610 million and will enable Qatar to produce nearly 4,000 tonnes per day of fertilizers.[38]

Weathering the Credit Crunch

Despite these successes, the latter half of 2009 nonetheless became something of a test of confidence for many of the Pacific Asian construction and labour companies, as several major projects in the Persian Gulf monarchies either ground to a halt or were put on indefinite hold due to the inability of governments or developers to refinance the loans they had taken out in order to launch the projects. The situation was assumed to be particularly serious for those private companies that could not rely on state-backing or other third part, assistance in order to tide them over until payments from their Persian Gulf clients recommenced. In some of these cases, the contracted companies and their workers were left unpaid for several months, and in one extreme example, a diplomatic crisis erupted, perhaps irrecoverably damaging relations and confidence between the two parties involved.

Notably, in mid-2009, Kuwait chose to cancel the construction of its new Al-Zour oil refinery, thus reneging on $9 billion worth of contracts signed with a South Korean triumvirate made up of SK Engineering and Construction, Daelim Industrial, and the GS Engineering and Construction Company.[39] Reported widely in the South Korean media, there was a deep concern that the incident was a bellwether for a wave of future cancellations in the emirate and perhaps elsewhere in the region. However, as the year progressed it became clearer that the Kuwaiti cancellation was an isolated event and that for the most part, the governments and parastatals in the Persian Gulf monarchies were only going to experience a short term blip in refinancing their debts. Moreover, most of the commissioned projects involving Pacific Asian construction companies were connected to the hydrocarbon industry, petrochemicals, or other heavy industrial sectors at the heart of long term government economic planning and therefore unlikely to be cancelled.

The exception to the rule was the emirate of Dubai, which had been awarding a large number of major real estate and tourism construction contracts to Pacific Asian companies since 2006. This had been made possible by the principal government owned developers massively extending themselves with loans acquired on international markets, often with short-term maturities. The exact extent of this debt is still unclear, but estimates have ranged from $105 billion to a staggering $290 billion.[40] Regardless of the exact figure, the exposure of these debts—most of which will mature over the next few years—was more than sufficient to burst the confidence bubble that had been building up in the emirate, and it has left the emirate's small number of citizens—of which there are probably less than 100,000[41]—with by far the worst debt per capita ratio in the world. In mid-2009, Dubai World's Nakheel developer cancelled without warning a $1.1 billion contract with South Korea's Samsung Engineering and Construction to build the 'Village Centre' on Palm Jumeirah—the first of Nakheel's ill-fated trilogy of manmade palm-shaped islands off the coast of Dubai.[42] But it was to be Japanese companies that suffered the most in the wake of collapsing Dubai's real estate-driven development model. Having apparently maintained a polite silence for several months, most likely in the belief that they would eventually get paid and would thus be well placed for future contracts, in November 2009, a number of Japanese companies chose finally to reveal that they were owed billions of dollars for work already done in Dubai, including their hard won contracts on the Palm Jumeirah and the Dubai Metro.

Among the companies worst affected was Mitsubishi Heavy Industries (MHI), part of the Mitsubishi Group, which had led a consortium of five companies (including three other Japanese companies—Mitsubishi Corporation, Obayashi Corporation, and Kajima Corporation)[43] in winning a $3.4 billion contract to construct the red line of the Dubai Metro and then had followed up by winning a secondary $1 billion contract to construct the metro's green line. Although the red line partially opened for service in September 2009, amid much fanfare and posturing from the Dubai authorities, who were keen to demonstrate that Dubai's infrastructure was world class,[44] the Japanese consortium was actually left unpaid. For the latter months of 2009, work was slowed down on the remaining parts of the metro in protest, with work only resuming in February 2010 following negotiations between the consortium and Dubai's Road and Transport Authority, the latter having been bailed out by the Dubai Department for Finance. There remains considerable concern, however, that the Dubai Department for Finance has sufficient funds to make up for future Road and Transport Authority shortfalls.[45] Japan's Tasei Corporation has also suffered from Dubai defaults, having been left unpaid for its building of the Doha Road close to the Burj Khalifa on the Arabian Ranches interchange. Moreover, the corporation's work for Nakheel was also mostly left unpaid in 2009. Tasei had been building the Gateway Towers and the tunnels at the entrance of Palm Jumeirah. It had also been building on Palm Jebel Ali—the second of the palm islands—in addition to the Almas Towers and Jumeirah Lake Towers. Furthermore, it was revealed that Tasei's work for Limitless—a subsidiary of Nakheel—was similarly unrewarded, despite the signing of a $400 million contract in 2007 for work that was supposed to be completed by 2010. By the close of 2009, Tasei was even owed payments for its construction of Nakheel's Djibouti Palace Hotel in the African state of Djibouti—another Dubai project financed by short term loans.[46]

It is clearer than before that Dubai's oil rich sister emirate in the United Arab Emirates—Abu Dhabi—will have to ensure that most of the delayed payments are eventually honoured,[47] as Abu Dhabi cannot afford to allow the UAE's international brand to suffer too greatly nor can it allow for instability to develop within one of the UAE's constituent emirates. Indeed, over the course of 2009, Abu Dhabi supplied some $20 billion in various bailout packages to Dubai, most of which has been channelled into ailing property developers so that they can pay off their most demanding creditors or their most frustrated contractors. It is now more likely than before that any international companies seeking contracts in the region will conduct more extensive due diligence on their future Persian Gulf partners. As such, although the Dubai crisis has caused a great shock and a loss of momentum for the Pacific Asian-Persian Gulf construction boom, it is nonetheless best viewed as a temporary problem and one that for the most part can lead to long term improvements in the business relationships developing between the two regions.

However, perhaps the most shocking result of the crisis and the one that will require the most extensive damage control was the rapid deterioration in diplomatic relations between the Japanese and Dubai governments, caused by the Japanese Consul-General to Dubai's accurate but rather abrupt statement published in an Abu Dhabi newspaper in early November 2009 that said 'some Japanese construction companies are facing very serious debt problems as Dubai won't pay.'[48] The comment provoked fury from the Dubai authorities, who were understandably trying to maintain an image of 'business as usual' despite their looming debt crisis, and were worried that other 'silent victims' of non-payments would also begin to voice their frustration. To make matters worse, only one day after the Consul-General's statement, the principal English language and government-subsidised Dubai newspaper, *Gulf News*, chose to print an opinion-editorial by its editor-in-chief that castigated the Japanese diplomat for his 'revelations.' It asked 'does his [the Consul-General's] job description as an accredited diplomat in this country really entitle him to publicly express such views? Or is he just meddling in something that is none of his business? I was surprised, and dismayed, by his utter violation of diplomatic norms and the special ties between Dubai and Japan in claiming that Japanese companies are owed billions of dollars by Dubai firms that, he added, they are not able to repay...why would he trespass and violate the norms and traditions of his job, which I believe is to issue entry visas?' Even more worryingly for Japan-Dubai relations, the editor concluded by urging 'the UAE Government to strongly condemn his [the Consul-General's] stance, and summon him and his boss, the ambassador, to protest against his reckless behaviour, and perhaps the UAE should declare him persona non grata.'[49]

7

AN ASIAN SECURITY UMBRELLA?

Surprisingly for many observers of the strengthening, multidimensional links between the Persian Gulf monarchies and the Pacific Asian economies, there is still no obvious security component to the interdependent relationship that is forming between the two regions. Despite having well-equipped modern militaries, the Gulf States are widely considered to be vulnerable given their rich energy resources, their close proximity to major conflicts and other potential threats, their small indigenous populations, and in some cases, their heavy reliance on expatriate servicemen.[1] Moreover, the Persian Gulf monarchies' longstanding dependency on a Western security umbrella is undoubtedly problematic, especially in the wake of the 11 September attacks, the Anglo-American liberation operations of Afghanistan and Iraq, and the recent Arab-Israeli conflagrations. These events have all strained relations between the Arab world and the United States and have eroded the traditional monarchies' much documented reliance on pan-Arab, Islamic, and anti-Israeli legitimacy resources.[2] Given their limited exposure to these Middle Eastern conflicts and religious divides, the Pacific Asian states would thus appear less politically problematic military partners for the Persian Gulf monarchies. Moreover, from the perspective of the Pacific Asian states, it would also seem to make sense for their militaries to seek a more active role in the security arrangements and defensive shields of their primary energy suppliers.

In the 1980s, there were a number of misread signs that China's military role in the Persian Gulf would soon increase. In an effort to build up its foreign currency reserves, China had already begun to transfer military technology to Iran, Iraq, Syria, and Libya,[3] and in 1984, China dispatched a large military delegation to Oman, to meet with the Sultanate's senior commanders. Although it did not lead to Oman purchasing any Chinese equipment, the meeting nonetheless gave Omani officials the opportunity to 'familiarise themselves with what was available in China and to broaden their knowledge.'[4] Most notably, in 1987 Saudi Arabia agreed to begin buying thirty-six Chinese CSS-2 Dong Feng-3 'East Wind' medium range ballistic missiles worth about $3 billion,[5] as part of a secret deal.[6] The following year Saudi Arabia appointed a former military officer as its first trade representative to China (who was upgraded to ambassador following the formalisation of diplomatic relations between the two countries in 1990). Analysts interpreted this, wrongly perhaps, as an effort by Riyadh to consolidate the deal.[7] Reportedly, China sold these missiles on the condition that Saudi Arabia would not be the first to use them in the event of conflict, and would not transfer any of the missiles' technologies to other states. It was also rumored that Saudi Arabia was asked to transfer US Patriot anti-missile system technologies to China as part of the agreement.[8] Temporarily at least, this arrangement made Saudi Arabia China's primary arms customer in the Middle East, ahead of Iran and Iraq.[9] In retrospect, however, the Dong Feng-3 purchase seems to have been primarily a retaliatory move by Saudi Arabia for being refused permission to acquire US-manufactured Lance missiles and about fifty US F-15 fighter jets. Certainly, Saudi Arabia only ever purchased twenty-five of the Dong Feng-3[10] and was unwilling to go further and purchase Chinese long-range intercontinental ballistic missiles, preferring to keep sourcing its ordinance from the US,[11] which had been supplying the kingdom continuously since the 1940s and had, of course, been the driving force behind the setting up of Aramco.[12] Perhaps even more galling for China was Kuwait's decision in 1984, following a rare rejection of a US arms sales proposal, to switch briefly to Soviet weaponry rather than Chinese.[13] Indeed, by 1988 it was evident that Chinese arms sales to the Persian Gulf monarchies had already peaked and had begun to tail off.[14]

In the late 1990s, there was some discussion of a revival of Chinese arms sales to the Gulf States, following the signing of a military cooperation agreement between China and Kuwait in 1995[15]—the first and only such formal agreement in place between China and a Persian Gulf monarchy. Later that year, the retired Saudi general Prince Khalid bin Sultan Al-Saud made two trips to Beijing to meet with China's minister for defence and the vice-chairman of China's Central Military Commission. Although it is unclear what matters were discussed, Khalid's visits were soon after reciprocated by the Chinese minister of defence, who was taken on a tour of Saudi military facilities, including the home of the Saudi Western Fleet. In 1996, as another follow-up to Khalid's mission, a Chinese delegation traveled to Saudi Arabia to meet with the commanders of the Saudi Arabian National Guard.[16] In 1998, a Chinese delegation led by the deputy chief of its armed forces visited both Qatar and Bahrain at the invitation of their respective armed forces, ostensibly to discuss China's potential role in training Qatari and Bahraini soldiers.[17] But perhaps most explicitly, in 1997 the president of a major Chinese arms consortium made a visit to Abu Dhabi. During the course of his stay in the United Arab Emirates, he stated quite clearly that China had ambitions to export weapons not only to Iran, but elsewhere in the region, explaining that 'we want to sell more missiles to Iran…right now we are not in talks with Iran but we are hoping to sell them anti-aircraft and sea defence missiles…we think there is a market for us in all of the Gulf States…we are not in talks with other countries in the area but we plan to make more visits to the Gulf in the future…'[18] In 2004 many analysts continued to predict fast growing Chinese military ties with the region, with one commentator arguing that 'there is every indication that China will continue to foster military links with the countries of West Asia, particularly with those which have oil and the hard currency to pay for their military hardware…China, therefore, is able to underwrite its strategic energy needs with bilateral arms agreements with the hydrocarbon exporters of the Gulf region.'[19] But again, any momentum seemed to fizzle out, with the Persian Gulf monarchies remaining with their trusted, albeit politically problematic Western suppliers.[20]

Certainly there has since been little further projection of Pacific Asian military power in the Persian Gulf. Most arms procurements are still sourced from Western manufacturers, with Saudi Arabia and the UAE having each purchased more than $15 billion of US arms in just the past two years, with most being spent on an advanced anti-missile system known as Terminal High-Altitude Area Defence, or THAAD.[21] Following an earlier massive purchase of eighty F-16 fighter jets from Lockheed Martin,[22] the UAE has now even begun to participate in US Air Force 'Red Flag' exercises by sending UAE Air Force pilots to train alongside their US counterparts at the Nellis airbase in Nevada.[23] Moreover, there remain a number of well entrenched US military bases in the Persian Gulf. Most notably, Qatar's Al-Udeid airbase houses a forward headquarters of the US Central Command along with a US Air Force expeditionary air wing. Similarly, nearby Bahrain continues to host a US Naval Support Activity Base which houses the US Naval Forces Central Command and the entire US Fifth Fleet. Although the US role in Kuwait has recently been downsized, there still exists at least four infantry bases, including Camp Patriot, which is believed to house about 3,000 US soldiers, and two air bases: Camp Ali Salem and Camp Al-Jaber. Although Britain's military role in the Persian Gulf was greatly reduced following the dismantling of its imperial protectorates in 1971, the Royal Air Force nonetheless continues to deploy an expeditionary air wing at Qatar's Al-Udeid base, and has its own desert air base at Thumrait in Oman.

The most recent example of the ongoing Western military presence was the May 2009 opening of a French air base at Dhafrah in Abu Dhabi and a new military quay at Port Zayed, the latter being dedicated for use by the French Navy. The late ruler of Abu Dhabi and the president of the UAE since its inception in 1971—Sheikh Zayed bin Sultan Al-Nahyan—had long forbidden the overt presence of Western servicemen in Abu Dhabi,[24] but following his death in 2004, his son and successor—Sheikh Khalifa bin Zayed Al-Nahyan— has seemed less concerned about disguising the UAE's military dependency on Western powers. If anything, the French base was inaugurated with considerable fanfare, with even President Nicolas Sarkozy being in attendance.[25] Soon the Western presence in the Persian Gulf monarchies will increase even further with the January 2010 announcement by the US Centcom commander, General David Petraeus, that at least four Gulf states were due to receive the latest US antimissile systems—new versions of the Patriot anti-missile batteries—in an effort to counter the impression that Iran was assuming a hegemonic military role in the region. Tellingly, Petraeus was unable to reveal exactly which states had agreed to deploy the US weapons, with one media report explaining that 'many countries in the Gulf region are hesitant to be publicly identified as accepting American military aid and the troops that come with it. In fact, the names of countries where the antimissile systems are deployed are classified, but many of them are an open secret.' It is thought that the unnamed states are Kuwait, the UAE, Qatar, and Bahrain, and that the US will now also keep Aegis cruisers equipped with early warning radar on patrol in the Persian Gulf at all times.[26]

Some commentators have argued that the Persian Gulf monarchies' lack of enthusiasm for a new or at least more diversified security relationship has at least three explanations. One is that the Pacific Asian states themselves see no credible alternative in the near future to Western-provided security in the region given that the thousands of miles of shipping lanes between themselves and their hydrocarbon suppliers would be so difficult and expensive to protect. As such, although it is not ideal that the US dominates the Persian Gulf and the Indian Ocean, it has nonetheless remained more practical and cost effective to rely on experienced Western navies, which have already invested in a multi-billion dollar capability for this purpose and enjoy access to a network of maritime bases in allied states.[27] In effect, therefore, Japan, China, and South Korea continue to benefit from subsidised security for their main supply routes. Another part of the explanation for the absence of a stronger security relationship is that the Persian Gulf monarchies do not yet see a reliable and proven alternative to the West, as, for all its accompanying political complications, it was a US-led alliance that liberated Kuwait in 1991 and it is a Western military presence that has since been credited with safeguarding the Persian Gulf from further Iraqi or Iranian belligerence.

The third component of the explanation is simply still some lingering distrust between the two regions, despite all of the aforementioned economic linkages and converging histories. This is not so much related to Japan, which has effectively been a neutral military power given an article of its post-war constitution which has restricted its armed forces to a self defence role,[28] and, as one Japanese analyst has described, given Japan's long held belief that demilitarisation is the only prospect of maintaining peace in the Persian Gulf.[29] But rather it is related to China, which has repeatedly generated political obstacles to a stronger security relationship with the Gulf States. A good example being China's temporary hostility to Saudi Arabia during the 1960s, when the former encouraged radical Arab groups, especially those in Yemen, in their conflict with the Al-Saud government.[30] Another example being Oman where for many of the older generation of Omanis, perhaps including their present ruler, Sultan Qabus bin Said Al-Said, it is still difficult to forget that China helped to sponsor Imam Ghalib bin Ali's revolutionary movement in the 1950s and early 1960s via its embassy in Cairo. Notably, in 1959, the Imam's deputy was invited to China to meet with the Beijing government and in 1962, the Chinese issued a statement expressing 'deepest respect for the Omani people and resolute support for their protracted and valiant resistance against British imperialist aggression' and describing the Imam's efforts as being 'wholly just' in struggling against 'British occupationalists.' Similarly, in 1967, two years after the Dhofar Liberation Front (DLF) had launched its rebellion in Oman's southern Dhofar province, the DLF's leadership was invited to Beijing for morale-boosting discussions. A promise was made to supply the DLF with weapons, and $35,000 in cash was given along with samples of Marxist literature written in Arabic. Although Chinese personnel did not serve in Dhofar, Chinese assistance continued to grow as the rebellion intensified, with food and medicine as well as weapons being supplied to the DLF.[31] By 1970, the DLF was believed to be completely dependent on Chinese support, a situation reflected in many of its leaders' statements, most of which contained positive references to Mao Zedong's political ideology and the necessity of replicating Chinese-style revolutions in the Persian Gulf monarchies. The newly installed Sultan Qabus responded by blocking all of China's attempts to establish diplomatic relations with Oman at the time.[32] In contrast to these destabilising Chinese maneuvers, Britain had, of course, played a key role in suppressing the rebels and preserving the Omani monarchy.[33]

Also generating distrust, during the Iran-Iraq War in the 1980s, China had voted against the United Nations Security Council's proposed resolution on sanctions against Iran and had proceeded to supply Iran with arms, despite already having supplied Iraq with arms and having over 20,000 of its workers based in Iraq at the time.[34] Indeed, in 1982 it was believed that 40 per cent of Iran's arms were being imported from China, and by 1987, over 70 per cent were from China.[35] In total, it was estimated that China sold $11–12 billion of arms to Iran and Iraq during the war, although Chinese officials denied such sales.[36] Understandably, China's duplicitous stance angered the Persian Gulf monarchies, most of which were cautiously aligned with Iraq, their fellow Arab state.[37] To make matters worse, China had been going to great lengths to demonstrate its neutrality, despite its role as a major arms dealer. At the outbreak of the war, an official Chinese communiqué from the president, Zhao Ziyang, had even stated of Iran and Iraq that 'we hope that they will settle their disputes peacefully through negotiations, guard against superpower interference, and prevent the situation from worsening…this is not only in the interests of the people of Iran and Iraq, but also conducive to peace and stability in the area.'[38] Moreover, when Iranian attacks commenced on Kuwaiti shipping at the height of the conflict—reportedly using Chinese-supplied Silkworm missiles—Kuwait had initially approached China to request that Kuwaiti ships be reflagged as Chinese ships for the duration of the conflict. Following a confusing refusal from China on the grounds that 'it did not maintain a large shipping fleet and thus had no spare tankers to lease,'[39] this left Kuwait with little option but to switch to US flagging.[40] Chinese missiles were also reportedly being used by Iran when Abu Dhabi's Abu-Bakush offshore oil platform was destroyed in 1986.[41] Soon after the war finished, China was also accused of supplying Iran with both Scud and Styx missiles and trying to ship chemical weapons to Iran via Dubai. Indeed, following US pressure, a suspect Chinese freighter—the *Yinhe*—was refused permission to dock in Dubai and was diverted to Saudi Arabia, although on that occasion the vessel was found to be empty.[42] In 1990, it was then reported that China had signed a secret nuclear cooperation agreement with Iran as part of a ten-year military technology transfer agreement. Soon after it was believed that Chinese nuclear specialists had begun to arrive at the Qazvin Nuclear Research Centre close to Tehran.[43]

Most seriously, despite enjoying an annual trade of over $700 million per annum with Kuwait by 1990 and, as previously mentioned, having nearly 20,000 workers based there, by the summer of that year China was unwilling to condemn openly Iraq's invasion of the emirate.[44] In part, this was due to the 5000 or more Chinese workers based in Iraq at that time, Iraq's 50 per cent share of China's total labour exports, thought to be worth about $670 million prior to the crisis,[45] and China's continuing arms sales to Iraq.[46] Thus, although Beijing had supported the first ten United Nations Security Council resolutions against Iraq, it refused to endorse UN Resolution 678, to actually go to war against Iraq, and thus refused to join the US-led coalition.[47] Even following a personal visit to Beijing by the exiled ruler of Kuwait, Sheikh Jaber Al-Ahmed Al-Sabah, in December 1990, the Chinese government reiterated its stance, stating that 'China would never change its principled stand against the Iraqi invasion and the occupation of Kuwait...and urged for peaceful restoration of Kuwait's independence.'[48] Moreover, to gain even indirect Chinese support for their forceful liberation of Kuwait in 1991, the US and Britain had to agree to lift those sanctions that had been imposed on China following the Tiananmen Square massacre just two years earlier—in 1989.[49] China's obstinacy over Iraq's inevitable expulsion led to a series of bitter disputes with the Persian Gulf monarchies, with the exiled Kuwait authorities unsurprisingly announcing that they would cancel $300 million of pre-arranged loans to China upon their country's eventual liberation. By the mid-1990s, the situation remained tense, with China threatening to vote against fresh United Nations Security Council sanctions against Iraq on the grounds of developing weapons of mass destruction,[50] and with it criticising the US for its airstrikes on Iraq in 1996.[51] Furthermore, there is evidence that Kuwait's purchase of nearly $300 million of Chinese howitzers in 1997 was a direct result of Chinese threats to soften its stance on Saddam Hussein unless Kuwait began spending,[52] although the Arab press reported at the time that the Chinese had simply beaten competition from the US, Britain, and South Africa.[53] Indeed, a Kuwaiti official later claimed that his government had been pressured into the Chinese arms deal,[54] as earlier that year the Chinese prime minister had begun to suggest that UN inspectors should settle for limited access to suspected weapons sites in Iraq, while other members of the Chinese government had expressed publicly their view that weapons of mass destruction did not exist in Iraq.[55]

In early 1998, when UN inspectors were again trying to enter Iraq, China once more discouraged the use of force and openly criticised those UN sanctions that were in place, on the grounds of humanitarian consideration. By the end of the decade, China was also voicing its criticism of the no-fly zones that had earlier been imposed in the north and south of Iraq, claiming they infringed upon Iraqi sovereignty.[56] This again was of concern to Kuwait, which viewed the southern no-fly zone as an important buffer from an aggressive neighbor. China's perceived increasing closeness to Israel—which it had officially recognized in 1992—was, by the late 1990s, also problematic for the Persian Gulf monarchies' anti-Israeli legitimacy platform, with the Israeli prime minister stating to a Chinese military delegation in 1998 that 'Israeli know-how is more valuable than Arab oil,'[57] and with Israel then believed to have sold a wide range of military software and related technologies, including Patriot anti-missile technology to China.[58] In 1999, accusations were also made that China's F-10 fighter aircraft bore a strong resemblance to Israel's prototype Lavi aircraft, and that Israel was also planning to supply China with its Phalcon airborne early warning radar equipment.[59]

The resulting strained relations between China and the Persian Gulf monarchies are thought to have been responsible for the stalling of several China-Kuwait joint ventures in the 1990s and a more cautious approach towards China elsewhere in the region. Tellingly, and no doubt in light of the many aforementioned high profile joint ventures that are now being developed by the two countries, China's ministry for foreign affairs is currently attempting to rewrite this troubled period of history with Kuwait and its neighbours by stating speciously in official documents that: 'during the Gulf crisis in 1990, China resolutely opposed Iraq's invasion and occupation of Kuwait and demanded that Iraq should withdraw its troops from Kuwait and restore and respect the independence, sovereignty and territorial integrity of Kuwait... both countries share identical or similar views on many major international and regional issues, constantly rendering sympathy and support to each other.'[60] Nonetheless, as the 2000s progressed and France and Russia took over from China to lead the opposition to the use military force against Iraq, China's position with the Persian Gulf monarchies genuinely became easier as it was able to shift out of the spotlight. Moreover, a number of very recent developments perhaps indicate the beginning of a new chapter in China's Persian Gulf security relationship. Although, as before, this may still prove to be another false start if the various obstacles cannot be overcome and sufficient enthusiasm on both sides cannot be generated.

One such indication came in the summer of 2009 when customs officials at India's Calcutta airport apprehended a UAE Air Force Hercules C-130 military transport aircraft, apparently en route to China. Indian customs officials were shocked to discover that the Hercules was laden with Chinese arms and apparently carrying missile parts and other 'military secrets.' While the incident undoubtedly caused embarrassment for the UAE and Chinese governments, with the latter accusing India of violating its diplomatic rights,[61] the aircraft's contents and its stated mission clearly pointed to an ongoing and seemingly friendly exchange of military technology between the UAE and China. What is less clear is which direction the technology was flowing, which should be of great concern to those Western governments that have been approving high technology arms sales to the UAE. Also in 2009, it became apparent that China was preparing to make naval deployments to the Persian Gulf, or at least to nearby waters. Early in the year, it was announced that China would despatch its largest ever naval expedition to the region—five groups of ships,[62] ostensibly in support of anti-pirate operations in the Gulf of Aden and off the coast of Somalia.[63] Crucially, the presence of this expedition was also used to test a new cooperative relationship with Oman when in the summer of 2009, China's *Zhousan* missile frigate entered Omani waters and docked at the southern port of Salalah for rest and refuelling.[64] Significantly, this was the first time that a Chinese naval vessel had officially entered the waters of a Gulf Cooperation Council state. Shortly after the Zhousan left Salalah, it took part in a joint naval exercise with the Russian Navy's antisubmarine warship *Admiral Tributs* off the coast of Oman—the first such Sino-Russian joint exercise held in the region.[65]

By March 2010 there was even stronger evidence of such Chinese naval interests when two Chinese ships—the frigate *Ma Anshan* and its supply vessel the *Qian Daohu*—sailed into Abu Dhabi's Port Zayed after completing a six month tour in the Gulf of Aden. Upon meeting the deputy chief of the UAE Navy, the Chinese senior captain stated that 'our friendly cooperation is not only in the interest of our people...but the friendly exchange between our navies is an important component of our bilateral relations,' while Abu Dhabi's English language newspaper *The National* described the development as 'long expected... a reflection of the country's [China's] growing capability to protect interests beyond its borders.' One editorial in the newspaper even stated that although the Chinese visit to Port Zayed may have been the 'first such visit, it is unlikely to be the last in the region...Beijing's deployment of a naval force in the Gulf of Aden...is only the forerunner of an expanding presence in the region... and the signs are that China's preoccupations with events immediately beyond its shores will give way to a more assertive presence on the world stage.'[66] From China's side, media analysis was similarly straightforward, with the Hong Kong daily *South China Morning Post* quoting one commentator as saying that the Chinese Navy's latest move 'fits perfectly with the strategy of using anti-piracy work for the broader goals of quietly building new strategic relationships...we can see a gradual but steady engagement at work, starting with trade and ending with the network of friendly places that they are certainly going to need if they are going to be able to realise their blue-water ambitions.'[67]

Furthermore, although it would seem that China's naval strategy is still not primarily one of controlling shipping lanes or guaranteeing the security of oil and gas being transported through the Strait of Hormuz, it is noteworthy that China has been rapidly expanding its three fleets—which now operate nearly 800 ships—and will soon acquire aircraft carriers.[68] China has also slowly been building up several proxy ports on the Indian Ocean rim as part of its 'string of pearls' strategy. While most of these, including Gwadar in Pakistan, which is discussed in detail later in this book,[69] Chittagong in Bangladesh, and a canal across Thailand, are undoubtedly aimed at facilitating Chinese international trade by allowing China to bypass the Straits of Malacca bottleneck—through which over 80 per cent of Chinese oil imports must pass—they will nonetheless also provide the Chinese Navy with future bases from which to project its power across to the Middle East. Notably, China has already begun to use the Coco Islands, which it leases from Myanmar, as a naval intelligence station, and it is building a naval base at Hambantota on the southern coast of Sri Lanka.[70] This trend has already caused some concern for India, which fears that the Gwadar port, in particular, may reduce both Indian and Western influence in the Indian Ocean. In 2008, the admiral of the Indian Navy even stated that 'being only 180 nautical miles from the exit of the Strait of Hormuz, Gwadar... would enable Pakistan to take control over the world energy jugular.'[71] In late 2009, a proposal was even posted on the Chinese Ministry of Defence's website by one of its admirals, Yin Zhou, suggesting that China should create a Middle Eastern base to 'strengthen its supply capacity.' Although no specific location was mentioned, most analysts agreed that a base in Yemen, on the Gulf of Aden, was most likely.[72]

In early 2010, there was also evidence that the Persian Gulf monarchies, or at least the UAE, were beginning to consider resuming direct arms and military equipment purchases from the Pacific Asian states. In part, this has been due to the specifications of components from Western suppliers, with the US having recently stalled any sales of its Joint Strike Fighter (JSF) to the UAE on the grounds that Israel also wishes to purchase the aircraft, reasoning that Israel would lose its qualitative air superiority in the region if the UAE was also allowed to buy the JSF.[73] Moreover, price is increasingly an issue. Following very shortly after the UAE's awarding of a major nuclear power contract to South Korea, as discussed in the final chapter,[74] the former entered into advanced discussions with Korea Aerospace Industries to acquire its competitively priced T-50 military jet trainer aircraft. Given that in early 2009 the UAE had originally chosen to purchase the Alenia Aermacchi M-346 aircraft, manufactured by Italy's Finmeccanica, the new interest in the T-50 represents a significant volte-face and a substantial boost for South Korea's nascent arms industry. Indeed, should the $1.4 billion deal be finalised, this will be South Korea's first major overseas sale of the T-50. As another possible ramification of the nuclear contract, it has also been reported that the UAE and South Korea intend to 'bolster their defence cooperation,' with the latter having promised to supply the former with ballistic missiles and electromagnetic pulse bombs, in addition to transferring 'unmanned-aerial-vehicle-related technologies.'[75] In 2010 it was also reported that the UAE was to be the first export customer for South Korea's new $14,000 K-11 Super Rifle. Although the initial order was only for forty of the weapons for test purposes, there is likely to be a much larger order placed by the end of the year

Together these recent developments are leading to a growing, albeit still limited, awareness in the US and other Western powers of the potential for Chinese or other Pacific Asian-Persian Gulf military collaboration. The United States National Intelligence Council has recently commissioned several studies to consider future Persian Gulf scenarios, some of which are specifically on the subject of China-Persian Gulf relations.[76] In the near future, it is likely that further such studies will be conducted, not only in the US, but also in Britain, France, and all other powers which currently enjoy a strong military relationship with the Persian Gulf monarchies, have strong vested interests in future economic collaboration, and continue to dominate arms sales to the region.

8

DIPLOMACY AND DIALOGUE

As this book has demonstrated, regardless of the various explanations and even some of the latest developments, the present reality is that the Persian Gulf monarchies do not yet have the same meaningful security alliances with their great Pacific Asian trade and investment partners that they have with their longstanding Western protectors. However, this is in no way jeopardizing their current and future closeness, with both clusters of countries now going to considerable lengths to improve many of the other, non-economic aspects of their interdependency. Indeed, there now appears to be a tacit understanding from both parties that their relationship simply need not contain a military security component, or at least that it is not necessary for the time being. Instead, it would seem, a focus on very regular and very high level diplomatic visits has become central to the strategies of both regions. While trade and other economic matters are certainly discussed at these carefully staged events, the meetings are nonetheless also perceived as valuable opportunities for heads of state and their ministers to convene with their counterparts and consider a range of other issues. Often substantial gifts or interest free loans are granted during these summits, clearly in an effort to build more sturdy political and cultural understandings, and undoubtedly to generate further goodwill.

In recent years, the frequency of these visits has greatly intensified, but more important has been the increase in the seniority of the visitors—especially those from the Persian Gulf traveling to Pacific Asia. The level is significantly high and is likely to now be higher on average than the rank of visitors dispatched to Western capitals. Indeed, as Japanese Ministry for Foreign Affairs officials have concurred, it is not so much the number of visits that matters but rather the seniority. Moreover, given that the Persian Gulf monarchies already have well-established relations with the Western powers, they need to invest much more in developing their relatively new relationships with Pacific Asia than with their more historic allies.[1] A report published by the United States' Middle East Institute in 2009 also identifies these trends, stating that there has been a 'steady, incremental process in the building of personal and institutional relations—the essential latticework of Gulf-Asia economic interdependence… [and the diplomatic visits] have been capped by a slew of ambitious cooperation programs and joint ventures.'[2]

Given their slightly longer history of economic relations, including the described programme of Japanese official development assistance,[3] it is not surprising that the Persian Gulf monarchies' closest political links to Pacific Asia are still with Japan. Although a functioning democracy, members of Japan's imperial family are regularly deployed in meetings with delegations from the Gulf States, along much the same lines as Britain, which often deploys members of its royal family—notably Prince Charles and Prince Andrew—for such occasions. This is a superficial advantage Japan holds over its neighbouring Pacific Asian republics.[4] A weakness in the relationship, however, is that the Japanese economy is becoming increasingly decentralised and, at least until recently, the government has been viewed as being concerned primarily with creating favourable conditions for the domestic economy, while leaving market forces and the private sector to dominate. In contrast, the Persian Gulf monarchies still for the most part have public sector-oriented economic systems dependent on centralised economic planning.[5] Particularly problematic are joint ventures, as these often involve Japanese private sector companies that require balanced accounts alongside Persian Gulf parastatals that can balance their accounts within the broader framework of their national economy.[6] This situation and the often resulting confusion prevails, despite Japan having launched its new National Energy Strategy in 2006 that specifically calls for stronger political and economic ties with resource rich states.[7] Ministry for Foreign Affairs officials have cited the problematic example of the Japan Bank for International Cooperation: ten years ago the JBIC could deal directly and swiftly with foreign partners, thus allowing for fast results. But now its powers are far more limited, thereby requiring Persian Gulf delegations to often meet with representatives of several Japanese banks in what has become an increasingly time consuming process.[8] However, on a more cultural front, Japan perhaps holds another advantage over its neighbours. Although the level of English language usage in Japan is poorer than in China or South Korea, which has undoubtedly stunted opportunities for educational and technological transfers—with one Japanese analyst stating that 'the educational and cultural relations are very poor...at a people-to-people level our mutual understanding is very limited'[9]—its relative steadfastness against the tide of globalising and Westernising forces is nonetheless viewed as attractive by some officials in the Persian Gulf monarchies. Indeed, many Gulf nationals are keen to preserve their indigenous culture, language, and religious customs, the erosion of which is prompting much debate. As such, Japan perhaps offers the Persian Gulf monarchies something of a role model, providing an alternative path towards Asian modernisation without necessarily having to succumb fully to Westernisation.[10]

Over the last twenty years, there have been twenty Japanese state visits to Saudi Arabia, including the serving prime minister on no less than five occasions: in 1990, 1995, 1997, 2003, and 2007. In the other direction, and over the same period, there have been 21 Saudi state visits to Japan, including the crown prince, Prince Abdullah bin Abdul-Aziz Al-Saud, in 1998 and the current crown prince, Prince Sultan bin Abdul-Aziz Al-Saud in 2006—forty-six years after his aforementioned first visit to Tokyo in 1960 as minister for defence. Japan has also dispatched nearly a thousand technical advisors to Saudi Arabia over this period—often pro bono—to assist in various Saudi projects. Relations between Japan and Kuwait have become similarly intense, perhaps as a result of increasing Chinese competition. Six Japanese state visits having been made to Kuwait since 2004, including the minister for foreign affairs in 2006, and with five Kuwaiti visits to Japan over the same period, including visits from prime minister, Sheikh Sabah Al-Ahmad Al-Jaber Al-Sabah, in 2004, and his successor, Sheikh Nasser Al-Muhammad Al-Ahmad Al-Sabah, in 2008. Moreover, Japan is presently providing in excess of $30 million in low interest loans to Kuwaiti companies, and nearly $1 billion of technical cooperation aid to various state-backed entities in Kuwait. On the cultural front, there has also been much activity, with the Japanese embassy in Kuwait having recently sponsored several events. In 2009, a gathering was held at the embassy for Kuwaiti students and other local fans to meet renowned Japanese manga artists—many of whom are idolised by aspiring Gulf national artists. After the Japanese artists signed their work for the fans, one of the Kuwaiti cinemas then held a screening of their latest movies.[11] Although there have been far fewer state visits between Japan and the United Arab Emirates, the seniority of these visits is nonetheless impressive and significant. There have recently been six Japanese state visits to the UAE, including the prime minister in 2007 and two former prime ministers in 2001 and 2009. Significantly, the 2007 visit coincided with a massive $3 billion loan being extended to the Abu Dhabi National Oil Company by JBIC. This in turn coincided with various Japanese oil companies signing five-year agreements with ADNOC to import an extra 120,000 barrels of oil per day to Japan.[12] In the other direction, there have been three UAE state visits to Japan, including the crown prince of Abu Dhabi, Sheikh Muhammad bin Zayed Al-Nahyan, and his brother the minister for foreign affairs, Sheikh Abdullah bin Zayed Al-Nahyan, who visited the Japanese prime minister and minister for foreign affairs in late 2007. And in 2009, Sheikh Abdullah returned to Japan on an independent visit.[13]

Over the past twenty years, there have been eleven Japanese state visits to Qatar, and although most of these were below ministerial level, Japanese prime ministers have nonetheless paid two visits, in 1988 and 2007. Over the same period, however, there have been a remarkable thirty-six Qatari state visits to Japan, most of which have taken place since Qatar began exporting natural gas to Japan. These visits have included three by Qatari rulers—in 1988, 1999, and 2005, two by the current ruler of Qatar's influential wife, Sheikha Moza bint Nassar Al-Misnad, in 2001 and 2005,[14] and one by the crown prince, Sheikh Tamim bin Hamad Al-Thani, in 2009.[15] In late 2009, Qatar's deputy prime minister and minister for energy and industry, Abdullah bin Hamad Al-Atti-yah, made an extensive and symbolic tour of Japan. He met with his counterpart, the Japanese minister for economy and trade, in Tokyo to discuss bilateral relations before visiting several chief executive officers of leading Japanese shipping companies, banks, and oil companies with an interest in Qatar.[16] In addition to sending diplomatic and economic delegations, Japan has provided Qatar with about $25 million in disaster relief and about $100 million in technical cooperation aid. Given that Qatar enjoys one of the highest gross domestic products per capita in the world,[17] this aid should be viewed as being primarily symbolic. Although there is not yet much evidence of cultural exchange between the two countries, this is likely to change in the near future. In 2009, for example, the Japanese embassy in Qatar organised a workshop on traditional Japanese art in collaboration with the Japanese school in Doha. The sponsored event involved Japanese artists instructing several Qatari artists and dozens of enthusiastic Qatari students.[18]

Between Japan and Oman, there have been eleven Japanese state visits to Oman over the past twenty years, including the prime minister in 1990 and the vice president of JBIC in 2004. In the other direction, there have been fourteen Omani state visits to Japan, including the deputy prime minister,

Sayid Fahd Mahmoud Al-Said, in 1997 and repeated visits from the Sultan's special advisor for economic affairs, Omar Abdur Munin Al-Zawawi, in 2002, 2004, and 2007. To smooth relations further, Japan has recently provided Oman with $1.4 billion in technical cooperation aid and $100 million in other grants. Unlike the abovementioned Japanese aid to the richer Persian Gulf monarchies of Kuwait and Qatar, these donations have been just as much practical as symbolic. Between Japan and Bahrain, the picture is again similar, though on a lesser scale. There have been sixteen Japanese state visits to Bahrain over the past twenty years, including the minister for foreign affairs in 1991 and 2006, while in the other direction there have been thirteen Bahraini state visits to Japan, including the crown prince, Sheikh Salman bin Hamad Al-Khalifa, in 2008. In recent years Japan, has also provided Bahrain with nearly $18 million in technical cooperation aid and other grants.[19] Perhaps as a reflection of Bahrain's relatively lowly status in Japanese eyes, there has yet to be a meeting between heads of state.

Although, as discussed earlier in this book,[20] China was initially much slower to establish diplomatic ties with the Persian Gulf monarchies and has since been slowed further by various political disagreements, in recent years, or at least since formal relations began, China's political relationship with the Gulf states would nonetheless seem to have become almost as strong as Japan's. Something of note has been the flow of aid between the two regions: with

Chart 8.1: Japanese state level visits to Persian Gulf monarchies
(over past twenty years)

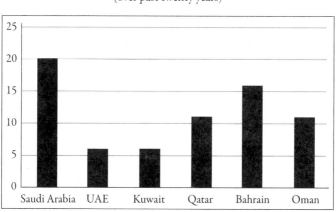

Source: Japanese Ministry for Foreign Affairs.

Chart 8.2: Persian Gulf monarchies' state level visits to Japan
(over past twenty years)

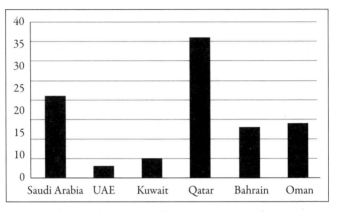

Source: Japanese Ministry for Foreign Affairs.

China having a much lower per capita wealth than Japan, the opportunities for the Persian Gulf monarchies to provide highly appreciated grants, loans and gifts to China has been much greater. Since the US invasion of Iraq in 2003 and the attempted export of Western-style democracy to the Persian Gulf, it has also been claimed that the surviving monarchies have become much more comfortable with China, as the latter is thought to be less likely to criticise their autocratic political structures, their dependency on migrant labour, and their well documented human rights abuses and repression of minorities.[21] Interestingly, the closest there has been to a conversation on human rights between China and a Persian Gulf monarchy was in 1999, when the ruler of Qatar met with the president of China. In the course of their discussion, the latter called for both countries to 'respect the universality of human rights...but stressed that safeguarding human rights should be combined with actual conditions in the country concerned...and they opposed the politicisation of the human rights issue and the practice of using related issues as a pretext for interfering in another country's internal affairs.'[22]

China does not of course have the advantage of having an imperial family, but its high-ranking Communist Party officials now appear to be serving in a similar role to Japanese royals when meeting members of Persian Gulf ruling families.[23] Also, unlike Japan and South Korea, China has—as previously discussed—a sizeable Muslim population, and its Ministry of Foreign Affairs regularly exploits this. Indeed, despite China remaining an avowedly atheist state,[24] official Chinese delegations to the Persian Gulf often deliberately include several Muslim delegates—usually led by a member of the China Islamic Association[25]—as do its delegations participating in most international conferences.[26] Undoubtedly, this has been part of an effort to build cultural bridges between China and the Gulf region, with one analyst even stating that 'the Chinese government ruthlessly uses its Muslim population as intermediaries in the [establishing of embassies] negotiations,'[27] while another has claimed that 'the Chinese government is willing to use its Muslims as stepping stones to reach the Muslim world.'[28] Either way, the strategy has worked, with Saudi newspaper editorials having inaccurately noted that 'China has moved towards Muslims and allowed them to perform their rites without any pressure or ideological rigidity; and it maintains distinctive stances towards Arabs and their causes...,'[29] while UAE newspapers have praised China for 'long advocating Arab and Muslim causes and taking a positive stand over the Arab-Israeli dispute and the issue of international peace.'[30] Similarly, Bahraini officials have stated to the Chinese media that 'through cultural contacts we can develop more friendship on a personal level between institutions and government officials.'[31] And now, with over 20 million Muslims living in China,[32] the potential for dispatching such culturally compatible delegations to the Persian Gulf is even greater than before. Tellingly, at the aforementioned inaugural Gulf Cooperation Council-China Business Forum held in Bahrain, it was not coincidental that of the four Chinese keynote speakers one was the provincial governor of the predominantly Muslim Ningxia province.[33]

Another often cited advantage for China is the manner in which its authoritarian political system is closely fused to its government planned economy.[34] This allows for decisions to be taken quickly, thus increasing China's attractiveness as a business partner for the Persian Gulf monarchies,[35] most of which favour fast confirmation for major projects and then speedy implementation. Significantly, even at an individual level, in many of the Persian Gulf monarchies local businessmen can now obtain a visit visa to China from a Chinese embassy in less than a day—this compares very favourably with European or North American embassies which can often take two or more weeks to approve and process such visas.[36] Moreover, as discussed earlier in this book, Chinese businessmen are finding it increasingly simple to visit certain Gulf States following a recent relaxation of regulations by China's National Tourism Administration.[37] In summer 2009, China even launched China Central TV in Arabic, known as CCTV-Arabic, which has been interpreted as a strong effort from China to play a more interventionist role in the Middle East, and most specifically the Persian Gulf, where the Chinese government intends to create a better impression of China's politics and culture for its major economic partners.[38]

With Saudi Arabia, China's ties have mushroomed over the past twenty years, with China having made eighteen state visits to Saudi Arabia, including the minister for foreign affairs in 1990,[39] and even the president in 1991 and 1999, with these two occasions being used to discuss, respectively, China's stance on the Kuwaiti crisis and how to form a new strategic partnership between China and Saudi Arabia.[40] In 2006, there was a second Chinese presidential visit to Saudi Arabia,[41] during which the president made a tour of Aramco's facilities and was greeted by several fluent Chinese speaking Saudi nationals, most of whom had been sponsored by the Saudi government to study in Chinese universities.[42] Clearly Saudi scholarships to China have not been restricted to technical and scientific studies, but have also involved language training. In the other direction, there have been over twenty Saudi state visits to China, commencing with the minister for foreign affairs, Prince Saud Al-Faisal Al-Saud, in 1990, and including the crown prince, Prince Abdullah bin Abdul-Aziz Al-Saud in 1998. Prince Abdullah's visit was thought to have focused on both the Iraqi disarmament question and the possibilities for a Saudi-China solution for the Israel-Palestine crisis.[43] Throughout the 1980s and 1990s, Chinese newspapers regularly translated interviews given by members of the Saudi ruling family, often supplementing the pieces with compliments on Saudi policies, especially those relating to building up the GCC.[44] Often the newspapers' editorials would stress that even though the two countries differed greatly in their ideologies and social systems, they nonetheless had much in common when it came to pursuing policies of neutrality and nonalignment.[45] In 1997, Saudi-Sino Friendship societies were established in both countries,[46] and in 2006, Abdullah returned to China to sign several new agreements that were intended to 'write a new chapter of friendly cooperation with China in the twenty-first century.' As a gesture of goodwill, he also agreed to grant China a substantial loan in order to build infrastructure in the oil-rich Xinjiang province.[47] Notably, this was Abdullah's first international trip as the newly installed King of Saudi Arabia—before visiting any Western states—and the president of China declared that the visit 'would begin a new phase in partnership between the two countries in the new century.'[48]

Relations between China and the UAE are becoming similarly close, with a number of key highlights. There have been eighteen Chinese state visits to the UAE over the past twenty years, including visits from the minister for foreign affairs and the deputy prime minister in 1989, 1993, and 1996, and a presidential visit in late 1989. Interestingly, the latter visit was part of Beijing's efforts to persuade the region that China was stable in the wake of the Tiananmen Square massacre.[49] In 1995, the president of Taiwan also visited the UAE, sparking outrage from Chinese diplomats, but it seems this visit was strictly private in nature and resulted from the president of Taiwan having been denied entry into Israel earlier that day. Tellingly, senior UAE officials did not greet him at the airport, and his visa entry stamp rather insultingly read 'Taiwan, province of China' in the nationality column.[50] In the other direction, there have been ten UAE state visits to China including, most notably, the long-serving ruler of Abu Dhabi and UAE president, Sheikh Zayed bin Sultan Al-Nahyan, who paid a five day visit in 1990, and the ruler of Sharjah, Sheikh Sultan bin Muhammad Al-Qasimi, who visited in 1991. This latter visit was noteworthy, given that Sheikh Sultan does not hold a formal role in the UAE federal government, and is best understood as an effort to gain Chinese support for the eventual liberation of the Sharjah island of Abu Musa, which has been occupied by Iran since 1971.[51] Indeed, the speaker of the UAE's Federal National Council later revealed this desire by stating to a visiting Chinese delegation that 'the UAE pays much attention to its relationship with China since the Asian giant plays an important role in the international arena...as a permanent member of the United Nations Security Council, China could push forward the unsettled territorial dispute between the UAE and Iran.'[52] In 2008, the ruler of Dubai and UAE vice president, Sheikh Muhammad bin Rashid Al-Maktum, also visited China.[53] This was actually his second state visit, as he had accompanied Sheikh Zayed to China in 1990. Upon meeting the president of China, Sheikh Muhammad was told that he was 'an old friend of the Chinese leadership and people...and he had played a major role in enhancing bilateral ties.'[54] Most recently, in summer 2009, Abu Dhabi's Crown Prince, Sheikh Muhammad bin Zayed Al-Nahyan, made a three-day visit to China.[55] In late 2009, the UAE's minister for foreign affairs, Sheikh Abdullah bin Zayed Al-Nahyan, placed a telephone call to China's minister for foreign affairs, to mark twenty-five years since the establishment of a Chinese embassy in the UAE. Importantly, Sheikh Abdullah also used the occasion to stress the strengthening of economic, political, and cultural ties between the two countries.[56] Other links include the many large donations to China following Sheikh Zayed's visit in 1990, including grants to establish an Arabic and Islamic Studies Centre at Beijing Foreign Studies University and, in 1993, the financing of the expansion of the printing factory of the China Islam Association. Sheikh Zayed also took the opportunity to grant China permission to set up UAE branches of the

Xinhua News Agency and the People's Daily newspaper.[57] Also of note is Zayed University's imminent establishment of a Confucius Institute as a result of an 'imaginative new partnership' that is being developed with China's Xinjiang University.[58]

Between China and Kuwait, there have been a number of comparable state level visits, with eleven Chinese visits to Kuwait in recent years, including the president in 1989—following on from his UAE visit—and the minister for foreign affairs in 1990 and 2000. The 1989 visit was perhaps responsible for the Kuwaiti press subsequently criticising the Western sanctions placed on China and calling the West to revisit their China policies.[59] From Kuwait, there have been thirteen visits to China, including the crown prince, Sheikh Saad Al-Abdullah Al-Sabah, in 1995, and two rulers of Kuwait on three separate occasions in 1990, 1991, and in 2009. Sheikh Jabah Al-Ahmad Al-Sabah's 1990 visit was made during his period of exile following the Iraqi invasion in an effort to try to strengthen Chinese support for the liberation campaign,[60] and his 1991 visit was made just three weeks before the liberation operation began as part of an effort to persuade China not to supply weapons to Iraq after the conflict was over.[61] Sheikh Sabah Al-Ahmad Al-Sabah's summer 2009 visit was made in support of the aforementioned $9 billion joint venture between the two countries, first set up in 2005. During this latter visit, Sheikh Sabah stated that 'these joint ventures and agreements will push Kuwait-China relations to an even higher level.' Kuwait has also historically been the most generous supplier of low interest loans to China, with the Kuwait Fund for Arab Economic Development (KFAED) having provided China with over $600 million in such loans since the early 1980s, including a $30 million soft loan in 1984 to help China build a hydroelectric power station in Fujian, a $13 million extension of credit in 1985 to finance the construction of a vehicle construction plant in Tianjin, a loan in 1988 to finance the Jinzhou Harbour project, a $10 million loan later that year to finance Yaoqiang Airport in Jinan, and a $28 million loan in 1989 to help China purchase equipment for the new Shenzen Airport.[62] In the 1990s, KFAED also loaned China $20 million to expand Ximan Airport, while total Kuwaiti loans to China for the decade were estimated at over $600 million.[63] There have also been several large gifts, including a disaster relief package in 1998 following a period of serious floods in China.[64] From China to Kuwait, there have also been a number of gifts, including the dispatching of firefighting equipment and environmental specialist teams to the emirate in summer 1991 to help control the numerous oil spillages and fires in the wake of Iraq's retreat.[65]

As with Japan, China's relations with the other Persian Gulf monarchies have been less substantial, but again there is strong evidence that the relationship is being taken very seriously by all parties and is undoubtedly tightening. Since diplomatic relations began, there have been nine Chinese state visits to Qatar, including the minister for foreign affairs in 1990 and the vice president in 1993.[66] In the other direction, there have been fourteen Qatari state visits to China, including the minister for foreign affairs in 1993, the ruler Sheikh Hamad bin Khalifah Al-Thani in 1999 and his wife Sheikha Moza bint Nassar Al-Misnad in 2001. Since then the prime minister, Sheikh Khalifa bin Hamad Al-Thani, visited China in late 2001, and the crown prince, Sheikh Tamim bin Hamad Al-Thani visited in 2008. In late 2009, Qatar's deputy prime minister and minister for energy and industry, Abdullah bin Hamad Al-Attiyah, visited Beijing to open Qatargas' first representative office in China. This visit was undoubtedly a reciprocal gesture to the China National Offshore Oil Corporation's aforementioned establishment of an office in Doha earlier in the year.[67] With China's described increasing reliance on Qatari gas imports, it is likely that the level of diplomatic activity will accelerate rapidly over the next few years and will most probably be accompanied by a variety of cultural and educational exchanges and linkages.

Between China and Oman, there have been nineteen Chinese state visits to Oman over the past twenty years, including the president in 1989, and the serving ministers for foreign affairs in 1993 and 2009. During the presidential visit, the streets of Muscat were reportedly decked with Chinese and Omani flags while thousands of Omanis cheered from behind barriers.[68] From Oman, there have been twenty-three visits to China over the same period, including six separate visits from the minister for foreign affairs, most recently Yousef bin Alawi in 2009. Many of the visits that took place early in this period were in support of the aforementioned oil trade that had begun between the two countries all the way back in 1983.[69] But not all were, with one trip leading to an agreement on 'exchanges of artists and folklore troupes,' while another was undertaken by the China Islam Association to mark the occasion of Oman's national day, and others led to agreements on youth exchanges, sports cooperation, civil aviation, and newspaper collaborations.[70] Symbolically, at about that time a 'ship of friendship'—the *Sohar*, named after Oman's ancient port city—set sail from Oman to China, and subsequent diplomatic missions have frequently made reference to this. More recently, a monument of the Sohar was erected in Guangzhou in southern China, and in 2001, Oman's ruler, Sultan Qabus bin Said Al-Said, donated $200,000 to assist the Guangzhou Museum

Chart 8.3: Chinese state level visits to the Persian Gulf monarchies
(over past twenty years)

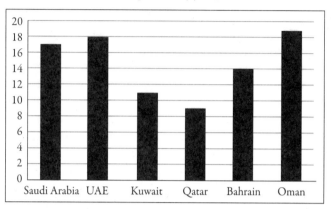

Source: Chinese Ministry for Foreign Affairs.

of Overseas History build a new Arab and Islamic exhibition room.[71] Since China commenced diplomatic relations with Bahrain, there have been fourteen Chinese state visits to Bahrain, including the minister for foreign affairs in 1990—the highest-ranking Chinese official to have ever visited the kingdom—just months after ambassadors were first exchanged. While there have

Chart 8.4: Persian Gulf monarchies' state level visits to China
(over past twenty years)

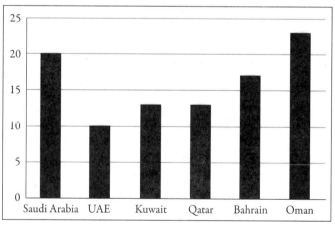

Source: Chinese Ministry for Foreign Affairs.

been seventeen Bahraini state visits to China, including the minister for foreign affairs in 1990, the prime minister Sheikh Khalifa bin Salman Al-Khalifa in 2002, and the King's wife Sheikha Sabika bint Ibrahim Al-Khalifa later the same year.[72]

South Korea is on much the same trajectory as its larger neighbours in strengthening its non-economic relations with the Persian Gulf monarchies. Although at present there is little evidence of loans, grants, and other donations, this is likely to increase, as already the level of senior diplomatic activity between these countries is intensifying. Like Japan, and unlike China, South Korea has a functioning democratic system, so cannot provide the Persian Gulf autocracies with the turning of a blind eye or any other comfort on this front. But crucially, like China and unlike Japan, South Korea is viewed as a highly attractive partner because it is president-led and the government is seen as being closely connected to the economy, again allowing for quick decisions, fast implementation, and state-led initiatives. However, as Japanese Ministry for Foreign Affairs officials have claimed, this advantage may not last much longer, as South Korea's economy is gradually becoming more decentralised.[73]

Over the past twenty years, South Korea made six state visits to Saudi Arabia, including the president on two occasions, most recently in 2007, and the prime minister on two occasions, most recently in 2005. In the other direction, Saudi Arabia has made seven state visits to South Korea, including the crown prince, Prince Abdullah bin Abdul-Aziz Al-Saud, in 1998. As with China, it is noteworthy that South Korea has also been admitting a large number of Saudi nationals to its universities, all of whom are sponsored by the Saudi government.[74] During the course of their studies, most gain some fluency in the Korean language. With the UAE there has, if anything, been even more diplomatic activity, with South Korea having made no less than fifteen recent state visits, half of them in the last five years, undoubtedly in support of the described South Korean construction contracts and—most crucially—the massive nuclear power plant contract, as discussed in the following chapter. These visits have included the president in 2006 and the prime minister in 2001, 2005, 2006, and in summer 2009. On the latter visit, the South Korean prime minister was hosted by the ruler of Dubai and UAE vice president, Sheikh Muhammad bin Rashid Al-Maktum. From the UAE, there have been five state-level visits over the same period, including Sheikh Muhammad in 2007, and the crown prince of Abu Dhabi, Sheikh Muhammad bin Zayed Al-Nahyan, in 2006.[75]

In the near future, it is probable that there will also be a number of educational linkages between the two countries, with the aforementioned plans to establish a joint venture in the semiconductor industry likely to lead to technology-related student and faculty exchanges between UAE and South Korean universities.[76] A number of the UAE's public secondary schools—all of which are suffering from very high drop-out rates—will begin to offer more advanced career guidance services, most likely using South Korean institutions as one of their best practise role models.[77] Moreover, there will also be an educational component to the nuclear deal, with the new Khalifa University of Science, Technology, and Research (KUSTAR) now cooperating with the Korea Advanced Institute of Science and Technology (KAIST) to provide the necessary technical and vocational training for Abu Dhabi-based staff involved in the nuclear industry and even to develop new high school curricula (which discusses nuclear power) for students in the UAE. Indeed, one Abu Dhabi spokesperson claimed that 'we are ensuring that opportunities are present for UAE nationals to join the nuclear education programme while they are still at school, as the developed curriculum will complement the nuclear energy program...the mutual cooperation between the UAE and South Korea will result in a multilateral academic cooperation that will directly contribute to preparing a qualified UAE workforce in the field of nuclear energy operation, whereby the implemented programme will be set bearing in mind that a preliminary energy programme will be taught at high schools.' Soon it is expected that the cooperation will also lead to exchanges between the two

Chart 8.5: South Korean state level visits to Persian Gulf monarchies (over past twenty years)

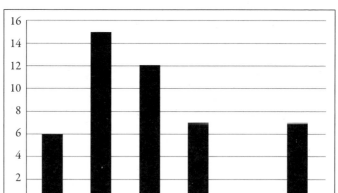

Source: South Korean Ministry for Foreign Affairs.

Chart 8.6: Persian Gulf monarchies' state level visits to South Korea
(over past twenty years)

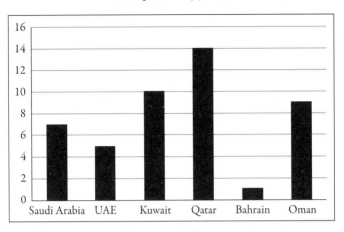

Source: South Korean Ministry for Foreign Affairs.

institutions and the provision of an even wider range of engineering instruction in the UAE, including robotics and nanotechnology. Certainly, KAIST's spokesperson was equally as optimistic as his Abu Dhabi counterparts, stating that 'this is indeed an exciting journey for us. We believe that KUSTAR will play a pivotal role in developing the science and technology sector of the UAE. KAIST is committed to working closely with this esteemed partner to develop further its educational and research programmes.'[78]

Between South Korea and Kuwait, there have been twelve South Korean state visits to Kuwait since formal relations began in 1979, including the president in 2007 and the prime minister in 2006. In the other direction, Kuwait has made ten state visits to South Korea, including the minister for foreign affairs in 2002 and the prime minister, Sheikh Sabah Al-Ahmad Al-Sabah, in 2004. With Qatar, South Korea has made seven state visits in recent years, including the president in 2007 and the prime minister in 2001 and 2005; while Qatar has made fourteen state visits to South Korea, including the ruler, Sheikh Hamad bin Khalifa Al-Thani, in 1999,[79] and the crown prince, Sheikh Tamim bin Hamad Al-Thani, in 2009.[80] In late 2009, South Korea's vice-minister for strategy and finance paid a highly symbolic visit to Doha to meet with Qatar's minister for economy and economic advisor to the ruler. In addition to construction contracts, the discussion also revolved around the aforementioned sukuk Islamic bonds in South Korea, Qatar's willingness to invest in South Korea, and South Korea's ability to export labour and human resources.[81] South Korea has made seven state visits to Oman in recent years, including the prime minister in 2001 and 2005; while Oman has made nine state visits to South Korea, although none have been above ministerial level. Between South Korea and Bahrain, there have been far fewer such visits, again a reflection of the lesser extent of economic interdependence between the two countries, although in 2007, Bahrain's minister for foreign affairs, Sheikh Khalid bin Ahmad Al-Khalifa, did travel to Seoul on a diplomatic and fact-finding mission.[82]

9

FUTURE INITIATIVES AND COLLABORATIONS

With the noted exception of military security arrangements, the relationship between the Persian Gulf monarchies and the three principal Pacific Asian economies will continue to strengthen rapidly on several fronts for the foreseeable future, provided that the former countries remain able to balance their existing relationships with the Western powers and Pacific Asia, especially China.[1] Thus far, such geopolitical competition would seem to have been avoided given the described emphasis on bilateral economic linkages, which for the most part have had little direct impact on the Persian Gulf's historic connections with the Western powers. As this book has demonstrated, the hydrocarbon and non-hydrocarbon trade between the two regions has been rapidly rising in volume and value, and is projected to continue doing so. Similarly, it has been shown that the flow of bilateral investments between the two regions continues to rise, and a substantial number of construction and labour contracts are being signed with an ever-greater frequency. These trajectories are all being enhanced by improving non-economic ties, especially at the diplomatic level, and, as discussed, it is likely these linkages will grow even tighter in the near future. Furthermore, the relationship will also be enhanced by several new initiatives and collaborations between the two regions which will take shape over the next few years. All of these will augment existing economic bonds, while some have implications for future non-military security arrangements, and while others are more physically symbolic of this twenty-first century partnership.

One such initiative has been the recent creation of proxy hydrocarbon reserves in Pacific Asian states on behalf of Persian Gulf oil and gas companies.

As described earlier in this book, Saudi Arabia and South Korea had already begun to explore such possibilities in the 1970s.[2] Although little further energy went into that specific project, in 2006, Saudi Arabia's minister for petroleum and petroleum resources, Ali Al-Naimi, resurrected the concept by visiting China to explore the feasibility of Aramco establishing a 30 million barrel storage facility on China's Hainan Island, in the South China Sea.[3] This venture has yet to advance much further, but it was nonetheless significant that during the initial discussions both delegations were keen to stress the mutual benefits: on the one hand, Saudi Arabia would gain another outlet for its exports while on the other hand, China would gain privileged, first pick access to Saudi oil.[4] More recently, Aramco has taken up a lease on storage facilities on Okinawa—Japan's southernmost island, close to Taiwan—in a move described by Saudi Arabia's minister for petroleum and mineral resources as necessary for feeding oil to the booming Asian market at a time when the kingdom's attention needs to shift eastwards: 'the goal is to have a commercially operated, administered operation that will make it more convenient for our customers in the region to utilise our supplies...the supplies will primarily go to Japan, South Korea, China, and the Philippines, in that order.'[5] Tellingly, at exactly the same time that the Okinawa lease was taken up, Aramco announced that it would end the lease for its storage facilities on the Dutch Caribbean island of Eustatius that had previously been used to ship oil to the United States.[6]

In the spring of 2009, the United Arab Emirates' Abu Dhabi National Oil Company began similar discussions to establish an Abu Dhabi crude oil reserve on Japanese territory in cooperation with Tokyo's Nippon Oil Corporation (NOC). These discussions have advanced much faster than Saudi Arabia's Hainan Island project and it is intended that ADNOC will begin such storage in mid-2010 by using one of NOC's existing reserve bases in Kagoshima in southern Japan. This agreement will provide the UAE with an alternative outlet for its crude oil sales, not only to Japan and its Pacific Asian neighbours, but to the entire East Asian region. Such an outlet may prove especially vital if the Strait of Hormuz—through which nearly three quarters of Japan's oil imports pass through[7]—was closed in the event of a conflict or emergency, or indeed if any of the other chokepoints along the shipping route between the two countries were closed. From Japan's perspective the agreement is doubly beneficial, as it would provide Japan with direct access and a pre-emptive right to purchase crude oil in the event of such an emergency. ADNOC's spokesperson stated that the arrangement would 'contribute to enhancing Abu Dhabi's relationship with Asian markets generally and Japan particularly, and will guarantee the flow of crude oil supplies to these markets in the situation of emergencies.'[8]

The future energy sector is another likely area of collaboration between the Persian Gulf monarchies and the Pacific Asian economies, with a number of countries from both regions now actively seeking to set up a range of solar, wind, and other alternative energy joint ventures. As early as 2006, the director of the Japan Cooperation Centre for the Middle East, Hideki Kono, visited Dubai specifically to explore such possibilities. During his visit he explained to Dubai and other UAE officials that 'Japan's traditional relationship with Arab countries has been based on importing oil and exporting electronic goods. We want to change that.'[9] Unsurprisingly, therefore, in early 2009, Japan began to play an active role in the UAE's nascent future energy sector: Tokyo's Softbank Investment Corporation Holdings (SBI) announced it was making an initial investment of $10 million into a joint venture with Abu Dhabi's Masdar City, which in turn is a high profile attempt by the emirate to build a carbon neutral city in its hinterland.[10] Specifically, the joint venture is under the umbrella of Masdar's Clean Energy Fund which will be targeting investments in companies specialising in solar and wind power. In the near future, SBI's level of investment in Masdar could rise to $200 million.[11] In parallel to these developments in Abu Dhabi, in spring 2009, Japan's Showa Shell Sekiyu announced that it was considering operating solar power plants in Saudi Arabia in cooperation with Aramco, which, as described, is now one of its principal shareholders. Showa intends to build small pilot plants in Saudi Arabia over the next few years in order to test out its technologies, and should these prove successful, then a joint venture with Aramco may be set up.[12] In January 2010, the likelihood of the joint venture increased greatly, following an announcement by the head of Saudi Arabia's United Nations climate negotiations team that his country was ruling out a nuclear energy programme and instead going to focus on solar energy plants that could eventually export electricity to neighbouring states.[13] Over the course of 2010, Japan's involvement in the sector will continue to intensify, with a delegation from the Ministry for Trade being sent to Abu Dhabi's trade fair on renewable energies to meet with both public and private sector representatives,[14] and with another Japanese delegation being dispatched to Qatar to discuss joint projects based on new energy conservation and renewable energy technologies that could help Qatar cut its greenhouse gas emissions and combat climate change.[15]

South Korea has now followed Japan's lead and has already put plans in place to cooperate with the Persian Gulf monarchies, or at least the UAE, in the future energy sector. In February 2009, the South Korean government established its own $72 million Masdar City-like clean energy fund, which aims to encourage private sector investment in such technologies, and announced that the nine state-owned energy companies would make a five-fold increase in investments in the sector over the next few years. Thus, unsurprisingly, discussions have since taken place between the South Korean Ministry for Knowledge Economy and Abu Dhabi's Mubadala Development Corporation (the investment vehicle responsible for setting up Masdar City and most of the joint ventures that underpin it) to implement South Korean technologies in new UAE-based joint ventures. Speaking on behalf of Abu Dhabi, Masdar City's chief executive officer, Sultan Al-Jaber, expressed his enthusiasm for working with South Korea, stating that 'we look forward to tapping into South Korea's strengths and forming strategic partnerships with academic, research, business and investment institutions from South Korea and to seeing South Korean entities become an integral part of the research and innovation that takes place in Masdar City.'[16] In early 2010, Al-Jaber also stated that South Korean firms are expected to provide 'smart grid and green energy' technologies for the project.[17]

Perhaps the most emblematic of the many new developments that will strengthen the link between the Pacific Asian economies and the Persian Gulf monarchies are, however, the physical improvements to the infrastructure that connects the two regions. In particular, the ongoing efforts to improve the old Karakoram Highway (KKH) between China and Pakistan, which was last upgraded in 1986. When completely restored, the KKH will effectively reconnect China to the Persian Gulf by providing an uninterrupted 1,300 kilometres land route—one of the longest in the world—that follows much the same path as the ancient Silk Road. It begins in the Chinese city of Kashgar before running through the Kunjerab pass in the Karakoram mountain range, close to the border of Tajikistan, before then reaching Islamabad and then continuing on through Pakistan. While most of the financing for the project is certainly derived from the Chinese government, which refers to the road in official communiqués as the as the 'Eastern Friendship Highway', it is argued that the highway is just as much a Pakistani initiative, as it allows the beleaguered Islamabad government some opportunity to counterbalance its heavy dependency on the US.[18] It has also created thousands of jobs for Pakistanis in relatively autonomous regions, thus increasing the government's influence in far flung provinces.

The construction of the highway has not only involved a massive engineering challenge with difficult terrain, but has even required the pacifying of local tribes in some of the most remote areas beyond the control of the Beijing and Islamabad governments.[19] Many of those working on the project have even described it as being the 'ninth wonder of the world' as a result of both the physical and political challenges that are being faced. Significantly, upon completion, this highway will connect via an additional highway through Saindak to deep water ports in southwestern Pakistan,[20] most notably the aforementioned port of Gwadar in Baluchistan which has direct access to the Gulf of Oman and lies just 250 miles from the Strait of Hormuz at the entrance to the Persian Gulf. Gwadar will also be connected to the KKH at Rawalpindi by a new Chinese-built railway—the Gwadar-Dalbandin Railway—in order to carry heavier Chinese goods along the final stretch of the journey. China has already invested at least $200 million in building Gwadar, with the port having first opened in 2007 with three berths, and with China having made additional investments in 2008 to expand it to ten berths and add a new bulk-cargo terminal.[21] In the near future, China will also develop a pipeline that will run in parallel to the KKH and will therefore stretch all the way from its industrial province of Xinjiang to Gwadar so as to facilitate the importing of oil from the Persian Gulf and its other major suppliers in Africa to China's key refineries. Now established as a tax free special economic zone (for at least a forty year period), and with its international airport being upgraded and a Chinese military facility under construction, Gwadar is thus likely to become China's chief re-exporting hub for the Persian Gulf region.

In parallel to China's growing interests in Gwadar, it is noteworthy that China's Tianjin Economic and Technological Development Area Company (TEDA) has now begun negotiations with the Egyptian government to help build a new Suez Economic Zone alongside the southern approaches to the Suez Canal. This is the result of several years of discussions on drafting the legal framework for the zone following a visit to Beijing by Egypt's president, Hosni Mubarak, in the late 1990s. If an agreement were reached, TEDA would likely take a 49 per cent stake (the maximum permitted for a foreign company under Egyptian law) in the $1.5 billion project. The plans include the establishing of a TEDA office in the zone by summer 2010 and for the zone to attract about $3.5 billion of Chinese investment within its first three years. With total foreign direct investment in Egypt at little more than $8 billion per annum, much of which is Chinese, this development will be a major boost for Egypt's economy and is intended to increase greatly employment opportunities in Egypt.[22] From China's perspective, de facto control over the new zone will provide its companies with another re-exporting hub on the periphery of the Persian Gulf.

Thus, in time the Gwadar and Suez developments may undermine Dubai's longstanding role as the premier regional entrepôt, or at the very least, they will offer serious alternatives for the high volume of Chinese goods that are currently re-exported through the emirate's two ports.

Nuclear Power and the South Korean Connection

The next, and by far the biggest future collaboration between the Persian Gulf monarchies and the Pacific Asian economies will be in the field of nuclear power. In 1989, it was reported that China had sold two experimental reactors to Saudi Arabia[23] and in 1991, it was alleged that China had shipped twelve nuclear warheads to Saudi Arabia. But these reports, along with another claim that Chinese nuclear experts were visiting a plant in Hama, Saudi Arabia, have remained unsubstantiated.[24] Indeed, it is only very recently that there has been significant impetus behind nuclear collaboration between the two regions. Thus far, the United Arab Emirates and South Korea have very much been the pioneers and, notwithstanding Saudi Arabia's apparent current lack of interest, it is likely that other Gulf States will soon seek to develop such relationships. Despite its vast hydrocarbon reserves, in recent years the UAE has been struggling to supply electricity to its rapidly expanding cities and the needs of its fast growing economy, especially the manufacturing and construction industries. UAE officials had already stated in 2008 that any further volumes of natural gas that could be made available to the domestic electricity sector would still be insufficient to meet the country's future needs, while oil and particularly coal-fired power generation would be environmentally and politically unacceptable, especially at a time when the UAE is trying to position itself as a regional if not global leader in future energies, as per the abovementioned Masdar City project. However, given the controversy being caused by nearby Iran also attempting to establish a civilian nuclear programme, albeit within minimal international cooperation, the UAE has been extremely careful with its nuclear ambitions, and has first sought to establish bilateral nuclear cooperation agreements with several of the world's major nuclear powers. This has been done not only to gain access to the necessary technologies, but also to appease the international community by demonstrating that the UAE is committed to the highest global standards and most stringent regulations. As such, in many ways the UAE has been one of the primary beneficiaries of the current United States-Iran nuclear standoff, as it has been able to position itself as a responsible and cooperative alternative to Iran's more unilateral approach, and thus something of a blueprint for other aspiring nuclear powers in the region.

Originally, it would seem that the UAE had intended to make Japan its primary partner, most likely due to Japan's described 2006 National Energy Strategy which had also called for the government's active support for the global development of Japan's nuclear energy companies. However, throughout 2006 and 2007, Japan apparently provided little encouragement and perhaps even discouragement to the Persian Gulf monarchies' nascent nuclear plans.[25] In early 2007, during the Japanese prime minister's visit to Qatar, the subject of nuclear cooperation was tentatively raised, but the Japanese delegation was reportedly unwilling to discuss the matter. But following a nuclear cooperation agreement between the UAE and France in January 2008 and another agreement between the UAE and Britain in May 2008, the Japanese government seemingly reversed its stance, possibly having sensed a missed opportunity. Indeed, in summer 2008, Japan's ambassador to Bahrain revealed Japan's willingness to discuss nuclear cooperation with Bahrain, and most significantly in December 2008, a UAE delegation was invited to Japan to meet with representatives from Hitachi, Toshiba, and Mitsubishi—Japan's three biggest nuclear engineering companies—and to tour their nuclear facilities.[26]

Duly, in January 2009, a bilateral agreement between the UAE and Japan was in place, with a special emphasis being placed on Japan's ability to provide training and management programmes for any Japanese-built UAE nuclear plants.[27] Perhaps even more symbolically, in the same month a preliminary agreement was signed between the UAE and the US, subject only to ratification from the US Congress.[28] This agreement had originally been drafted by the George W. Bush administration and then followed up by the incoming Barack Obama administration. Unexpectedly for some observers, the UAE then pressed for further such agreements and in June 2009, a similar bilateral pact was signed with South Korea.[29] Immediately after signing, a twenty-strong UAE delegation of engineers was then dispatched to South Korea—at the invitation of the state-owned Korea Electric Power Corporation—to survey its nuclear facilities and especially its safety procedures and mechanisms. With the five international technology transfer accords in place, or at least all except the pending ratification of the US agreement, the UAE then began to invite international consortia to bid for its nuclear contract. This was to comprise of four light water 1,300 megawatt reactors—three to be built in Abu Dhabi and one to be built in the Indian Ocean emirate of Fujairah between 2012 and

2017—with the total package being valued at $20.4 billion.[30] Eventually three groups were short-listed. For several months, a French consortium was considered the favourite as it comprised of the nuclear power plant veterans Électricité de France (EDF), Gaz de France-Suez (GDF-Suez), and Total, along with nuclear engineering giants Areva, Vinci, and Alstom. The other contenders were a US-Japanese consortium made up of General Electric and Hitachi, and a South Korean-led consortium made up of KEPCO along with Samsung Corporation, Hyundai, and Doosan Heavy Industries. Importantly, the South Korean group also included some US and Japanese interests, with Westinghouse Electric (a unit of Toshiba) being included.[31]

Again erring on the side of caution given the ongoing international condemnation of Iran's nuclear programme, the UAE delayed an announcement of the winning bid, preferring to wait for the US Congress to ratify the original January 2009 UAE-US agreement. As the year progressed, the ratification became increasingly uncertain, as in April 2009 opposition to the agreement from a number of congressmen and women began to rise following the broadcasting of a video on ABC News and several other US networks that depicted a member of the Abu Dhabi ruling family and owner of the aforementioned Pearl Properties, Sheikh Issa bin Zayed Al-Nahyan—one of the ruler's eighteen half brothers—apparently torturing his victims with the aid of uniformed Abu Dhabi policemen.[32] It soon became apparent that the video had been circulating for several months,[33] yet the UAE authorities were reluctant to bring Sheikh Issa to trial given his privileged status. This led to serious criticism within Congress and elsewhere in the US on the grounds that if the UAE was unable to uphold the rule of law and bring all of its citizens to justice, then it could not be a credible international nuclear partner and was not fit to receive sensitive US technologies.[34] Notably, James McGovern, co-chair of the House Committee on Human Rights called for the US to 'place a temporary hold on further expenditures of funds, training, sales or transfer of equipment or technology, including nuclear, until a full review of the matter could be completed.'[35] By summer 2009, opposition to the nuclear agreement intensified, with the Sheikh Issa scandal being compounded by fears that the UAE was not only geographically proximate to Iran but that at least two of its constituent emirates enjoyed warm economic and political relations with Iran. In particular, allegations were made that the crown prince and de facto ruler of the northern emirate of Ra's Al-Khaimah along with his chief advisor were heavily involved in a number of Iranian manufacturing businesses.[36] These fears were seemingly sufficient to cancel Ra's al-Khaimah's planned hosting of the

32nd America's Cup sailboat race in February 2010, with a US court ruling that the proposed UAE venue was 'illegitimate and unsafe'.[37]

Nonetheless, following vigorous lobbying from the US-UAE Business Council—a commercial interest group founded and funded by several Abu Dhabi and Dubai parastatals, along with several US companies with an interest in UAE contracts including Boeing, General Dynamics, and Halliburton[38]—the UAE's human rights failings and perceived Iran vulnerabilities were eventually discounted, and on 17 November 2009, the US Congress finally approved the legislation and the agreement went into effect. The UAE was then in a position to set up the Emirates Nuclear Energy Corporation (ENEC), which moved to finalise the nuclear contract. On 27 December 2009 ENEC's chairman, Khaldun bin Khalifa Al-Mubarak (who also serves as the chairman of the Abu Dhabi Executive Affairs Authority and is widely considered to be the crown prince's most senior advisor) announced that 'following a comprehensive and detailed review of three excellent bids from some of the world's top nuclear suppliers, operators and construction firms, ENEC has determined that the KEPCO team is best equipped to fulfil the government's partnership requirements in this ambitious programme.'[39]

Many observers had predicted that either the French or US-Japanese consortia would be successful given those countries' experience in building nuclear plants and longstanding economic relations with the UAE. The US-UAE Business Council had even begun to print and distribute glossy brochures detailing the number of jobs that would be created in the US—10,000—as a result of the deal. These predictions were based on three core assumptions. Firstly, that the Western and Japanese companies had been building nuclear plants since the 1970s,[40] whereas as recently as the 1990s, South Korean companies were, in some cases, still being disqualified from international engineering contracts on the grounds of inexperience of undertaking technically complex projects,[41] despite South Korea having constructed its first nuclear plant over thirty years ago.[42] Secondly, France had signed a number of recent high profile agreements with the UAE, including the aforementioned establishing of a military base in the western province of Abu Dhabi in 2009, the recent opening of a branch of La Sorbonne University, and the planned opening of a branch of the Louvre museum on Abu Dhabi's Saadiyat Island by 2013. France's Areva Company had also already built a number of installations in the UAE, including power and desalination plants. Thirdly, much was read into the fact that the UAE had allowed the French and US-Japanese consortia to have several opportunities to revise their prices downwards over the course of the year, thus giving them the chance to come closer to the South Korean price, which was likely much lower.[43] Indeed, it was reported that the South Korean price was several billion dollars less than the best French price,[44] mainly as a result of its APR-1400, being at least 20 per cent cheaper to manufacture.[45]

However, these lines of thought grossly underestimated the rapidly increasing economic interdependence between the UAE and South Korea, as demonstrated throughout this book. As described, the latter is an almost 100 per cent net energy importer, while the UAE has risen to become its second greatest oil and gas supplier. Moreover, since 2003, when Samsung Engineering and Construction began work on the Abu Dhabi Investment Authority's new headquarters, South Korean companies have, as discussed, been a major and visible presence in the UAE's construction industry, and are regularly backed by strong diplomatic support from their government. Indeed, the nuclear plant construction contract was deemed so lucrative to South Korea that its prime minister visited Abu Dhabi in summer 2009 specifically to support the KEPCO-led consortium,[46] and in November 2009, the South Korean minister for foreign affairs met with the crown prince of Abu Dhabi, Sheikh Muhammad bin Zayed Al-Nahyan, to stress again the benefits to the UAE of awarding the contract to South Korea. Tellingly, perhaps, following the minister for foreign affairs' return to Seoul, many of the South Korean newspapers began reporting that the KEPCO consortium had become the 'surprise favourite' to win.[47]

After the victory, the news was greeted by strong applause in South Korea, where it was deemed likely that the South Korean-led consortium was now best placed to win several subsequent UAE contracts including a sixty-year maintenance contract for the first wave of nuclear power plants, and a contract to construct four additional power plants, which will probably be worth an extra $20 billion. In total, it was estimated that the UAE venture would create over 100,000 jobs for South Koreans and UAE nationals. Shares in South Korean companies rose sharply—with Doosan Heavy Industries reaching the 15 per cent limit for a daily rise—and ebullient statements were made in the domestic media regarding the 'new strategic partnership between South Korea and the UAE.'[48] The South Korean financial sector is also due to enjoy something of a fillip over the next few years as a result of the deal, with a number of companies—led by Korea Eximbank—assuming responsibility for securing financing for the many smaller manufacturing and technical companies in South Korea that will also be contributing to the project. Indeed, on the basis of the nuclear deal, Korea Eximbank was already confident of being able to secure over $50 million on global capital markets on behalf of such South Korean companies over the first half of 2010.[49]

On the domestic political level, the gains for South Korea have also been enormous. The South Korean president received an overnight 7 per cent boost in his approval ratings after the deal was announced, taking him to over 53 per cent, and with his personal role in supporting the deal being hailed in the domestic media as evidence of his 'pragmatic diplomacy.'[50] In the UAE, the president and ruler of Abu Dhabi, Sheikh Khalifa bin Zayed Al-Nahyan, stated of the contract that 'our relationship with South Korea, which has seen sustained growth in recent years, has ushered in a new era which will serve the interests of the two countries.' He also went further, beyond the nuclear contract, explaining that the UAE now looks forward to 'a successful development experience and transferring economic know-how from South Korea, particularly in the areas of technology, industry and technical fields through joint investment projects.' Representing ENEC, Al-Mubarak supported these far-reaching statements, explaining that the nuclear contract would 'fix the relationship between the two countries well into the future... the nature of this project will require a partnership that endures for nearly 100 years.'[51] Certainly with the described maintenance contracts, the UAE-South Korean nuclear relationship is likely to remain at the centre of both countries' economies for several decades.

South Korea's success has undoubtedly signalled to the US, Britain, and France, that it is a serious competitor for contracts in the Persian Gulf, in both the nascent nuclear sector and far beyond. After all, the $20.4 billion UAE deal was by far the largest single contract awarded by any of the Persian Gulf monarchies in 2009, including even the defence sector, and it is probably also the largest contract to have ever been awarded in the region.[52] Furthermore, it will very likely raise South Korea's chances of securing nuclear contracts in other parts of the world, with Turkey's envoy to Seoul having already indicated that the UAE deal has strengthened South Korea's bid to construct nuclear plants on the Black Sea coastline.[53] Should South Korea win this deal, it could be worth another $20 billion for South Korean companies. In early 2010, following a visit to South Korea's Gori nuclear plant, Lithuania's minister for defence similarly indicated that South Korea was well placed to win his country's forthcoming nuclear contract, and very recently, the Korea Atomic Energy Research Institute was chosen to build Jordan's first nuclear research reactor at the Jordan University of Science and Technology, worth $170 million. With this success, South Korea is likely to be the favourite to win any future Jordanian civilian nuclear power contract.[54]

For South Korea's Pacific Asian neighbours, the UAE deal may now act as a useful catalyst, with Japan and China being likely to respond much faster to new strategies—nuclear or otherwise—being developed in the Persian Gulf in the near future. Certainly, should Qatar or another Gulf state re-approach Japan with a proposed nuclear project over the next few years, the reception would undoubtedly be much warmer than before. Since its historic victory in the summer 2009 general election, the Democratic Party of Japan (DPJ) has repeatedly stressed its commitment to making Japan a world leader in nuclear energy,[55] and there is little doubt within the walls of Tokyo's Ministry for Foreign Affairs that the Persian Gulf is now viewed as the region with the most potential demand. In early 2010, it was even reported by Japan's state-run NHK news that the country was considering forming a special committee in partnership with the US in order to boost its ability to export nuclear power plant technology as part of an 'all-out effort to win coveted bids in the emerging economies of Asia and the Middle East.'[56]

CONCLUSION

By the end of the twentieth century, with rapidly accelerating demand from increasingly resource-scarce China and South Korea, and sustained demand from Japan, the Pacific Asian economies had all become heavily dependent on oil and gas imports, with most being sourced from the Persian Gulf monarchies. Now, more than ever, this massive and lucrative hydrocarbon trade represents the central pillar in the strengthening relationship between the two regions and, as demonstrated, is presently worth hundreds of billions of dollars per annum. In the near future, it is likely this trade will amount to trillions of dollars per annum. Significantly, few efforts are being made by either side to disguise their increasing dependency on the other, with the bulk of future Persian Gulf hydrocarbon exporting capacity being earmarked for Pacific Asian buyers. This contrasts markedly with other hydrocarbon importing economies, especially in the West, where most often an emphasis is placed on diversifying supplies wherever possible. Although on a much smaller scale than the oil and gas trade, it is also important to note how rapidly the non-hydrocarbon trade between the two regions is also growing. In something of a twenty-first century reincarnation of the ancient Silk Road, the Persian Gulf monarchies are importing ever-increasing quantities of textiles, machinery, automobiles, and electrical products from the Pacific Asian economies, while in the other direction, the Gulf states have augmented their hydrocarbon exports by selling increasing volumes of metals, plastics, and petrochemicals. With a host of new initiatives from all of the governments and business communities concerned, together with considerable relaxations on visa requirements and other erstwhile restrictions, it is becoming much easier than before for merchants from both regions to travel and take their business from one side of Asia to the other.

In parallel to these intensifying trade links, the relationship between the Persian Gulf monarchies and the Pacific Asian economies is being strengthened even further by a massive flow of investments. These investments are in both directions and at all levels, with most being managed by giant government-backed sovereign wealth funds; although the bulk of these investments are still associated with the hydrocarbon industry, there are however strong signs that an increasingly diverse range of non-hydrocarbon joint ventures are also being pursued. Such opportunities are finally providing the Persian Gulf monarchies with a realistic and more hospitable alternative to the more mature Western economies for their overseas investments and interests. Such alternatives have been deemed particularly necessary following the 11 September 2001 attacks on New York's World Trade Center, after which many Western governments and companies did little to disguise their distrust of Gulf sovereign wealth funds, with some of the more xenophobic commentators having argued that Gulf investments were not merely commercial and that power politics would eventually be involved. Moreover, with strong opposition within the United States Congress to Dubai Ports World's attempted takeover of several US ports in 2006, there was another urgent reminder that the Western economies were no longer the most cordial investment environment.

Although Pacific Asian construction companies have been winning contracts in the Persian Gulf for some time, it is significant that over the last few years there has been a marked increase in their success. Many of the most recent contracts have been to both build and supply the labour for multi-billion dollar developments and, significantly, in many cases the successful Japanese, Chinese, and South Korean companies have had to compete against Arab and Western companies, most of which have enjoyed a much longer history of winning contracts in the region and have usually sourced their labour from South Asia. Even though Chinese and other Pacific Asian labour often comes at a slightly higher cost than labour from India, Pakistan, or Bangladesh, it is increasingly viewed as less problematic by the governments in the Persian Gulf monarchies, as the presence of thousands of non-Muslim and non-Arabic speaking Pacific Asian labourers is not thought to pose a significant security threat to these states.

Despite these intensifying connections between the two regions, a meaningful security arrangement has yet to develop, despite the obvious advantages to both the Persian Gulf monarchies—which have to balance their reliance on Western support with often contradictory domestic sentiments, and the Pacific Asian economies—which need to secure their energy supply routes. If anything, the Western powers have increased their military presence in the Persian Gulf in recent years, with new bases being established and ever-increasing sales of sophisticated weaponry to their most demanding customers. In part, this has been due to a history of distrust, with the Persian Gulf monarchies preferring to seek support from the same reliable protectors that preserved their integrity during the Iran-Iraq War of the 1980s and orchestrated the liberation of Kuwait in 1991. Moreover, there is undoubtedly a feeling on both sides that their increasing economic interdependency does not yet warrant a security dimension as long as the Western powers continue to guarantee—and thereby subsidise—the safety of their shipping routes and supply lines. However, there are a number of recent indicators that the Pacific Asian states, especially China and to a lesser extent Japan, are beginning to assume a more active role in the broader region's security environment.

Without a strong security component to their relationship, the Persian Gulf monarchies and the Pacific Asian economies have all gone to considerable lengths to shore up a number of other, non-trade aspects of their interdependency. In particular, there has been a strong focus on aid, grants, and other donations, even if only for symbolic purposes. Moreover, there has been a marked increase in the frequency and seniority of diplomatic visits, with most now being at a far more senior level than the delegations sent to Western powers. While economic and trade matters remain at the heart of these meetings, a broad range of other issues are discussed, and strong efforts are being made to generate the most effective cultural and educational linkages. Furthermore, the increasingly interdependent and multi-dimensional relationship between the two regions is also being enhanced by several new initiatives and collaborations that will take shape over the next few years. These include innovative hydrocarbon storage projects, investments in renewable energies, further improvements to pan-Asian physical trade infrastructure, and the construction and technology transfer of civilian nuclear power from Pacific Asia to the Persian Gulf. All of these developments will augment existing economic bonds, while some may even have an impact on future security arrangements.

The intensifying connection between the two regions also has several broader implications. The lack of significant military collaboration has certainly allowed the US and other Western powers to remain in their role as the ultimate protectors of the Persian Gulf and the guarantors of the international oil industry's most strategic shipping lanes. This has kept to a minimum any tension between the US and China, with the latter regarded by most observers as being the most militaristic of the Pacific Asian states. Given time, however, this will likely change as the Pacific Asian states gradually seek greater influence over their primary energy suppliers. Furthermore, the many other linkages between the Persian Gulf and Pacific Asia described in this book, including the various economic and diplomatic ties, and perhaps especially the raft of new initiatives and collaborations, will undoubtedly prompt the US and other powers to pay more attention to this new pan-Asian relationship. Such increased attention, if mishandled and too heavy-handed, may in turn reduce trust between the Persian Gulf monarchies and their Western allies and partners, thus providing a fresh wave of opportunities for Pacific Asian governments and companies to win lucrative contracts and thus increase their influence even further.

NOTES

INTRODUCTION

1. See for example Funabashi, Yoichi. 'The Asianization of Asia' in *Foreign Affairs*, Dec. 1993.

2. Ehteshami, Anoushivaran. 'Asian Geostrategic Realities and their Impact on Middle East-Asia Relations' in Ehteshami, Anoushivaran, and Carter, Hannah (eds), *The Middle East's Relations with Asia and Russia*, London: Routledge, 2004, p. 133. Ehteshami discusses the five poles of the international system and predicts that future developments will lead to bilateral ties between some of the non-western poles.

3. Ibid., p. 134. Writing in 1992, Ehteshami describes them, somewhat apologetically, as the 'bit or layer in the middle of the world economy.'

4. Ayubi, Nazih N., 'OPEC and the Third World: The Case of Arab Aid' in Stookey, Robert W. (ed.), *The Arabian Peninsula: Zone of Ferment*, Stanford: Hoover Institution Press, 1984, p. 134.

5. The Al-Saud dynasty.

6. The UAE in turn is made up of seven monarchical dynasties: the Al-Nahyan of Abu Dhabi, the Al-Maktum of Dubai, the Al-Qasimi of Sharjah, the Al-Qasimi of Ra's al-Khaimah, the Al-Nuaymi of Ajman, the Al-Mualla of Umm al-Qawain, and the Al-Sharqi of Fujairah.

7. The Al-Sabah dynasty.

8. The Al-Thani dynasty.

9. The Al-Khalifa dynasty.

10. The Al-Said dynasty.

11. *The Guardian*, 7 Apr. 2009; *Deutsche Presse*, 24 Jun. 2009. In April 2009, the World Bank predicted that China would secure a growth rate of 6.5 per cent in 2009 and will therefore help to pull the Pacific-Asian region out of its recession. In June 2009, the Organization for Economic Cooperation and Development (OECD) made similar predictions for China, and forecast that Japan would return to growth in early 2010.

12. *Arab News*, 7 May 2009. Quoting Nicholas Janardhan.

13. Calabrese, John. 'From Flyswatters to Silkworms: The Evolution of China's Role in West Asia' in *Asian Survey*, vol. 30, 1990.

14. Calabrese, John. *China's changing relations with the Middle East*, New York: Pinter, 1991.

15. Davies, Charles E (ed.), *Global Interests in the Arab Gulf*, Exeter: University of Exeter Press, 1992.

16. Ishida, Susumu. 'Japan's Oil Strategy in the Gulf without Arms Deals' in Davies, 1992.

17. Ehteshami, Anoushivaran. 'The Rise and Convergence of the "Middle" in the World Economy: The Case of the NICs and the Gulf States' in Davies, 1992.

18. For a full discussion, see Dillon, Michael. 'The Middle East and China' in Ehteshami and Carter, 2004, p. 42. The book's title in Chinese being *Zou Xiang Zhongdong: Zinjiang due Xiya Zhuguo Kaifang Zhanlue Yanjitu*.

19. Rubin, Barry. 'China's Middle East Strategy' in *China Report*, vol. 34, 1998.

20. Calabrese, John. 'China and the Persian Gulf: Energy and Security' in *Middle East Journal*, vol. 52, no. 3, 1998.

21. Bin Huwaidin, Muhammed. *China's Relations with Arabia and the Gulf, 1949–1999*, London: Routledge, 2002.

22. Bin Huwaidin, Muhammed. 'Determinants of Saudi Arabia's Foreign Policy Toward China' in *Journal of Strategic Studies*, vol. 3, no. 7, 2007. pp. 27–36.

23. Ehteshami and Carter, *The Middle East's Relations with Asia and Russia*, 2004.

24. Ehteshami, 'Asian Geostrategic Realities and their Impact on Middle East-Asia Relations', 2004.

25. Dillon, 'The Middle East and China', 2004.

26. Lee, Henry, and Shalmon, Dan. 'Searching for Oil: China's Oil Initiatives in the Middle East' discussion paper published by the Environment and Natural Resources Program, Belfer Center for Science and International Affairs Discussion Paper, Harvard University, Jan. 2007

27. Yetiv, Steve A. and Lu, Chunlong. 'China, Global Energy, and the Middle East' in *Middle East Journal*, vol. 61, no. 2, 2007.

28. Miyagi, Yukiko. *Japan's Middle East Security Policy*, London: Routledge, 2008.

29. Ghafour, Mahmoud. 'China's Policy in the Persian Gulf' in *Middle East Policy*, vol. 16, no. 2, 2009.

30. Calabrese, John. 'The Consolidation of Gulf-Asia Relations: Washington Tuned in or Out of Touch?' policy brief published by the Middle East Institute, Washington DC, Jun. 2009.

31. Stott, David A., 'Japan and the United Arab Emirates: A Nuclear Family?' in *The Asia-Pacific Journal*, vol. 33, Aug. 2009.

32. Simpfendorfer, Ben. *The New Silk Road: How a Rising Arab World is Turning Away from the West and Rediscovering China*, London: Palgrave, 2009.

1. HISTORICAL BACKGROUND

1. Ishida, Susumu. 'Japan's Oil Strategy in the Gulf without Arms Deals' in Davies, Charles E. (ed.), *Global Interests in the Arab Gulf*, Exeter: University of Exeter Press, 1992, p. 179.

2. For a greater discussion see Onley, James. *The Arabian Frontier of the British Raj: Merchants, Rulers, and the British in the Nineteenth-Century Gulf*, Oxford: Oxford University Press, 2007.

3. The concession duly ended in early 2000.

4. Ishida, 'Japan's Oil Strategy in the Gulf without Arms Deals', p. 183.

5. Ministry for Foreign Affairs (Japan) 2009, Overview file on Saudi Arabia.

6. Ishida, 'Japan's Oil Strategy in the Gulf without Arms Deals', pp. 182; 191. 82 per cent of Japanese oil supplies were sourced from the Persian Gulf in the 1969–1973 period, although some of this was accounted for by imports from Iran.

7. Before their independence in 1971, there were nine Trucial States: Bahrain, Qatar, Abu Dhabi, Dubai, Sharjah, Ra's al-Khaimah, Ajman, Umm al-Qawain, and Fujairah.

8. Davidson, Christopher M., *Dubai: The Vulnerability of Success*, New York: Columbia University Press, 2008, p. 19.

9. Ibid., pp. 67–91.

10. Buxani, Ram. *Taking the High Road*, Dubai: Motivate, 2003, pp. 109–110; 118; Davidson, *Dubai*, p. 70.

11. These personal stereos from Dubai were so popular with Keralites that they became known as 'Malbaris'; Davidson, *Dubai*, p. 313.

12. Buxani, *Taking the High Road*, pp. 117–119; 121; Davidson, *Dubai*, p. 71. In 1982 demand for television sets was very high as many households wished to watch the Asian games being held in New Delhi that year.

13. Personal interviews, Dubai, Apr. 2008.

14. Ministry for Foreign Affairs (Japan), Overview files on Saudi Arabia, the UAE, Kuwait, Qatar, Oman, and Bahrain, 2009. Also see Davidson, Christopher M. *Abu Dhabi: Oil and Beyond*, New York: Columbia University Press, 2009, pp. 54–58.

15. CIA World Factbook 2009, Economics overview of Kuwait.

16. Personal interviews, London, Mar. 2010; KISR press release on institutional history, 2010.

17. Abu Dhabi Marine Operating Company, Historical background documents, 2009.

18. Ishida, 'Japan's Oil Strategy in the Gulf without Arms Deals', p. 185; 200.

19. Yetiv, Steve A. and Lu, Chunlong. 'China, Global Energy, and the Middle East' in *Middle East Journal*, vol. 61, no. 2, 2007, p. 199.

20. Bin Huwaidin, Muhammed. *China's Relations with Arabia and the Gulf, 1949–1999*, London: Routledge, 2002, pp. 96–97.

21. Ministry for Foreign Affairs (China), Overview files on the UAE, Kuwait, and Qatar, 2009.
22. Bin Huwaidin, *China's Relations with Arabia and the Gulf, 1949–1999*, p. 98.
23. See chapter seven.
24. Bin Huwaidin, *China's Relations with Arabia and the Gulf, 1949–1999*, p. 188.
25. Yetiv and Lu, 'China, Global Energy, and the Middle East', p. 201.
26. Bin Huwaidin, *China's Relations with Arabia and the Gulf, 1949–1999*, pp. 98–99.
27. Ibid., p. 189.
28. Ministry for Foreign Affairs (China) 2009, Overview files on the UAE, Kuwait, and Oman. Also see Dillon, Michael, 'The Middle East and China' in Ehteshami, Anoushivaran, and Carter, Hannah (eds). *The Middle East's Relations with Asia and Russia*, London: Routledge, 2004.
29. Bin Huwaidin, *China's Relations with Arabia and the Gulf, 1949–1999*, p. 217.
30. For a full discussion, see Westad, O. (ed.), *Brothers in Arms: The Rise and Fall of the Sino-Soviet Alliance, 1945–1963*, Stanford: Stanford University Press, 1998.
31. These statements appeared in *Peking Review* in 1973. See Bin Huwaidin, *China's Relations with Arabia and the Gulf, 1949–1999*, p. 192.
32. The Great Proletarian Cultural Revolution began in 1966 and ended in 1976.
33. Bin Huwaidin, *China's Relations with Arabia and the Gulf, 1949–1999*, pp. 107, 192.
34. The four modernisations were in the fields of agriculture, industry, technology, and defence. The aim was to make China into a great economic power by the early twenty-first century. See Evans, Richard, *Deng Xiaoping and the Making of Modern China*, London: Penguin, 1995.
35. Yetiv and Lu, 'China, Global Energy, and the Middle East', p. 201.
36. Dillion, 'The Middle East and China', p. 50.
37. Ministry for Foreign Affairs (China), Overview files on the UAE, Kuwait, and Oman, 2009.
38. However, in 1981 Chinese and Saudi sports delegations had met each other in Malaysia. Bin Huwaidin, p. 217; Yetiv and Lu, p. 202.
39. Bin Huwaidin, *China's Relations with Arabia and the Gulf*, p. 218.
40. Ibid. p. 252.
41. Yetiv and Lu, 'China, Global Energy, and the Middle East', p. 202.
42. Bin Huwaidin, *China's Relations with Arabia and the Gulf, 1949–1999*, p. 238.
43. Ibid., p. 204. Quoting *People's Daily* from 1978.
44. Bin Huwaidin, *China's Relations with Arabia and the Gulf, 1949–1999*, p. 206.
45. Ghafour, Mahmoud, 'China's Policy in the Persian Gulf' in *Middle East Policy*, vol. 16, no. 2, 2009, pp. 87; 89.
46. Bin Huwaidin, *China's Relations with Arabia and the Gulf, 1949–1999*, p. 192.
47. Ibid., p. 220.
48. Ibid., p. 242; Personal interviews, Dubai, Dec. 2009.
49. Dillion, 'The Middle East and China', pp. 42–43; 48.

50. Bin Huwaidin, *China's Relations with Arabia and the Gulf, 1949–1999*, p. 224.
51. Ministry for Foreign Affairs (China). Overview files on Saudi Arabia, Qatar, and Bahrain, 2009
52. Calabrese, John, 'China and the Persian Gulf: Energy and Security' in *Middle East Journal*, vol. 52, no. 3, 1998, p. 359.
53. Bin Huwaidin, *China's Relations with Arabia and the Gulf, 1949–1999*, p. 228.
54. Ibid., p. 119.
55. Ibid., p. 223.
56. See chapter seven.
57. Bin Huwaidin, *China's Relations with Arabia and the Gulf, 1949–1999*, p. 218.
58. Ibid., p. 219.
59. For example, S-Oil Corporation was established in 1977. S-Oil. Historical background documents, 2009.
60. *Korea Times*, 19 Feb. 2010.
61. Ehteshami, Anoushivaran, 'The Rise and Convergence of the "Middle" in the World Economy: The Case of the NICs and the Gulf States' in Davies, *Global Interests in the Arab Gulf*, p. 146.
62. Ibid., p. 147.
63. Ministry for Foreign Affairs (South Korea), Overview files on Saudi Arabia, the UAE, Kuwait, Qatar, Oman, and Bahrain, 2009.

2. ECONOMIC AND DEMOGRAPHIC COMPARISON

1. Saxonhouse, Gary, and Stern, Robert (eds), *Japan's Lost Decade: Origins, Consequences and Prospects for Recovery*, London: Wiley, 2004.
2. There are now frequent references to the 'Chinese Century' in leading international broadsheets and magazines. See for example, *New York Times*, 4 Jul. 2004; *Time Magazine*, 22 Jan. 2007; *The Times*, 3 Jan. 2005.
3. Asian Development Bank estimates, as cited by the *Xinhua News Agency*, 22 Sept. 2009.
4. In the early 1970s, China's population growth rate was close to 3 per cent. World Bank, World Development Indicators, 2009.
5. Chinese National Bureau of Statistics, 2009. Organization for Economic Cooperation and Development country overviews, 2009. International Monetary Fund country overviews, 2009.
6. CIA World Factbook. People and economics overviews of Japan, China, South Korea, Saudi Arabia, the UAE, Kuwait, Qatar, Oman, and Bahrain. Statistics from 2007–2008, with 2009 population estimates. Supplementary data from the International Monetary Fund, World Bank, and OECD country overviews, 2009.
7. Ibid.
8. Sovereign Wealth Fund Institute. Overview document on largest funds by assets under management, 2009; Saudi Arabia Market Information Resource and Directory. Historical background on SAMA Foreign Holdings, 2009.

3. THE HYDROCARBON TRADE

1. See table 3.1.
2. For a full discussion, see Vivoda, Vlado. 'Diversification of Oil Import Sources and Energy Security: A Key Strategy or an Elusive Objective?' in *Energy Policy*, vol. 37, no. 11, 2009.
3. *Financial Times*, 21 Feb. 2010. For a discussion on the role of the Caspian Sea, see Ehteshami, Anoushivaran, 'Asian Geostrategic Realities and their Impact on Middles East-Asia Relations' in Ehteshami, and Carter (eds), *The Middle East's Relations with Asia and Russia*, p. 11.
4. *Financial Times*, 21 Feb. 2010.
5. Niblock, Tim. Speaking at the 'China in the Arab World and Emerging East Asia-Middle East Nexus' conference, Durham University, 29 Sept. 2009; *Financial Times*, 21 Feb. 2010.
6. CIA World Factbook, 2009, Economics overviews on Saudi Arabia, the UAE, Kuwait, Qatar, Oman, and Bahrain, 2007 and 2008 estimates, Author calculations for totals.
7. CIA World Factbook, 2009, Economics overviews on Saudi Arabia, the UAE, Kuwait, Qatar, Oman, and Bahrain, 2007 and 2008 estimates, Author calculations for totals.
8. CIA World Factbook, 2009, Economics overviews on Saudi Arabia, the UAE, Kuwait, Qatar, Oman, and Bahrain, 2007 and 2008 estimates, Author calculations for totals.
9. British Petroleum Statistical Review, Jun. 2008.
10. US Energy Information Administration (EIA), Qatar profile, 2009.
11. Lee, Henry, and Shalmon, Dan. 'Searching for Oil: China's Oil Initiatives in the Middle East' discussion paper published by the Environment and Natural Resources Program, Belfer Center for Science and International Affairs Discussion Paper, Harvard University, Jan. 2007, p. 9.
12. EIA, 2009; CIA World Factbook, 2009.
13. Ibid.
14. Ibid.
15. *Financial Times*, 21 Feb. 2010.
16. CIA World Factbook, 2009, Economics overviews on China.
17. For example, the new finds in the East China Sea and the Sichuan Basin. See *China Post*, 18 Jan. 2010; *China Daily*, 27 May 2007.
18. Lee and Shalmon, 'Searching for Oil: China's Oil Initiatives in the Middle East', pp. 3; 9; 22.
19. CIA World Factbook, 2009, Economics overviews on Japan, China, and South Korea, 2006–2008 estimates. Author calculations for totals.
20. CIA World Factbook, 2009, Economics overviews on the US, China, Japan, India, Russia, Germany, Brazil, Saudi Arabia, and South Korea, 2007 and 2008 estimates.

21. CIA World Factbook, 2009, Economics overviews on the US, China, Japan, India, Russia, Germany, Iran, France, and South Korea, 2007 and 2008 estimates.

22. *The National*, 5 Aug. 2009.

23. Ishida, 'Japan's Oil Strategy in the Gulf without Arms Deals', p. 181.

24. *The National*, 9 Nov. 2009.

25. Ministry for Foreign Affairs (Japan), Overview file on Saudi Arabia, 2009.

26. *Saudi Gazette*, 22 Jul. 2009.

27. *The National*, 26 Jun. 2009.

28. CIA World Factbook, 2009, Economics overviews on Saudi Arabia, the UAE, Kuwait, Qatar, Oman, and Bahrain. 2007 and 2008 estimates, Author calculations for totals. Also see British Petroleum Statistical Review, June 2008.

29. Davidson, *Abu Dhabi*, pp. 69–72.

30. Ministry for Foreign Affairs (Japan), Overview file on the UAE, 2009.

31. *The National*, 9 Nov. 2009.

32. Davidson, *Abu Dhabi*, pp. 69–72.

33. Ministry for Finance and Industry (UAE), Overview file on trade with Japan, 2009.

34. *The National*, 26 Jun. 2009.

35. See chapter nine.

36. Stott, David A., 'Japan and the United Arab Emirates: A Nuclear Family?' in *The Asia-Pacific Journal*, vol. 33, Aug. 2009, p. 7.

37. *The National*, 28 Jul. 2009.

38. Ministry for Finance and Industry (UAE), Overview file on trade with Japan, 2009.

39. Ministry for Foreign Affairs (Japan), Overview file on the Kuwait, Qatar, Oman, and Bahrain, 2009.

40. Ghafour, Mahmoud. 'China's Policy in the Persian Gulf' in *Middle East Policy*, vol. 16, no. 2, 2009, pp. 83–84.

41. Lee and Shalmon, 'Searching for Oil: China's Oil Initiatives in the Middle East', p. 2.

42. Ibid.

43. Dillon, Michael. 'The Middle East and China' in Ehteshami and Carter (eds), *The Middle East's Relations with Asia and Russia*, p. 55.

44. Yetiv, Steve A. and Lu, Chunlong. 'China, Global Energy, and the Middle East' in *Middle East Journal*, vol. 61, no. 2, 2007, p. 199.

45. Dillion, 'The Middle East and China', p. 56.

46. Lee and Shalmon, 'Searching for Oil: China's Oil Initiatives in the Middle East', p. 2.

47. *International Herald Tribune*, 2 Oct. 2006.

48. Ghafour, 'China's Policy in the Persian Gulf', pp. 82–83.

49. Ibid., p. 82; Lee and Shalmon, 'Searching for Oil', pp. 3; 9; 22.

50. Calabrese, John. 'The Consolidation of Gulf-Asia Relations: Washington Tuned in or Out of Touch?' policy brief published by the Middle East Institute, Washington DC, June 2009, p. 2.

51. EIA, International Energy Outlook, 2009.

52. CIA World Factbook, 2009, Economics overview on China. Based on 2008 estimates.

53. Ghafour, 'China's Policy in the Persian Gulf', p. 83.

54. *Financial Times*, 21 Feb. 2010.

55. Yetiv and Lu, 'China, Global Energy, and the Middle East', p. 203.

56. *New York Times*, 19 Mar. 2010.

57. Ibid.

58. Lee and Shalmon, 'Searching for Oil', pp. 3; 9; 22.

59. Ghafour, 'China's Policy in the Persian Gulf', pp. 87–88.

60. Yetiv and Lu, 'China, Global Energy, and the Middle East', p. 205.

61. *Reuters*, 15 Nov. 2009.

62. *Saudi Gazette*, 21 Nov. 2009.

63. Ghafour, 'China's Policy in the Persian Gulf', pp. 87–88.

64. *Reuters*, 15 Nov. 2009.

65. Ministry for Foreign Affairs (China), Overview file on the UAE, 2009; Ghafour, 'China's Policy in the Persian Gulf', p. 89.

66. See chapter one.

67. Ministry for Foreign Affairs (China), Overview file on Oman, 2009; Ghafour, 'China's Policy in the Persian Gulf', p. 89.

68. Bin Huwaidin, *China's Relations with Arabia and the Gulf, 1949–1999*, p. 211.

69. Ibid., p. 210.

70. Lee and Shalmon, 'Searching for Oil', pp. 3; 9; 22.

71. *Gulf Times*, 21 Nov. 2009.

72. Bin Huwaidin, *China's Relations with Arabia and the Gulf, 1949–1999*, p. 254.

73. Ministry for Foreign Affairs (China). Overview files on Kuwait, Qatar, and Bahrain, 2009; Ghafour, 'China's Policy in the Persian Gulf', p. 89.

74. *MenaFN*, 10 Mar. 2009.

75. *Gulf News*, 14 Nov. 2009.

76. Personal interviews, Ras Laffan, Jan. 2010.

77. *Financial Times*, 28 Oct. 2009.

78. *MenaFN*, 29 Oct. 2009.

79. *Reuters*, 31 Oct. 2009.

80. *Financial Times*, 28 Oct. 2009.

81. Ministry for Foreign Affairs (South Korea), Overview files on Saudi Arabia and the UAE, 2009; Stott, David A. 'South Korea's Global Nuclear Ambitions' in *The Asia-Pacific Journal*, vol. 12, Mar. 2010.

82. Especially in the fields of construction and nuclear power collaboration. See chapters six and nine.

83. *The National*, 5 Aug. 2009.

84. Ministry for Foreign Affairs (South Korea), Overview files on Kuwait, Qatar, Oman, and Bahrain, 2009.

4. THE NON-HYDROCARBON TRADE

1. See chapter 8; *New Yorker*, 15 Jun. 2009, quoting Ben Simpfendorfer.

2. Author calculations based on subsequently listed country totals.

3. Ehteshami, 'The Rise and Convergence of the "Middle" in the World Economy'.

4. For a discussion of Dubai's diversification, see Davidson, *Dubai*, pp. 99–135. For a discussion of Abu Dhabi's diversification, see Davidson, *Abu Dhabi*, pp. 69–94.

5. Davidson, Christopher M., *The United Arab Emirates: A Study in Survival*, Boulder: Lynne Rienner Press, 2005, pp. 123–127.

6. Ishida, 'Japan's Oil Strategy in the Gulf without Arms Deals', p. 185.

7. Davidson, *The United Arab Emirates*, pp. 256–262.

8. Ibid.

9. JETRO Dubai press release, 2010.

10. Davidson, *Dubai*, pp. 70–71; Davidson, *The United Arab Emirates*, pp. 72–73.

11. CIA World Factbook, 2009. Economics overview on the UAE, 2008 estimates.

12. Davidson, *Abu Dhabi*, pp. 77–80; *Gulf News*, 26 Feb. 2010.

13. Ministry for Foreign Affairs (Japan), Overview file on the UAE, 2009; *Gulf News*, 26 Feb. 2010.

14. *Gulf News*, 26 Feb. 2010.

15. *Saudi Gazette*, 22 Jul. 2009.

16. Ministry for Foreign Affairs (Japan), Overview file on Saudi Arabia, 2009.

17. *Saudi Gazette*, 18 Nov. 2009.

18. Ministry for Foreign Affairs (Japan), Overview file on Saudi Arabia, 2009.

19. *Saudi Gazette*, 22 Jul. 2009.

20. *Qatari Peninsula*, 19 Nov. 2009.

21. *Oman Times*, 17 Nov. 2009.

22. Ministry for Foreign Affairs (Japan), Overview files on Kuwait, Qatar, Oman, and Bahrain, 2009.

23. *Gulf Daily News*, 29 Jul. 2009.

24. *Gulf Daily News*, 24 Jul. 2009.

25. *Gulf Daily News*, 29 Jul. 2009.

26. A free trade agreement being a measure to link a free trade area of two or more countries that have agreed to eliminate tariffs, quotas and preferences on most (if not all) goods and services traded between them.

27. *Gulf Daily News*, 29 Jul. 2009.

28. *Japan Times*, 7 Apr. 2006.

29. Ministry for Foreign Affairs (Japan), Overview files on Saudi Arabia, the UAE, Kuwait, Qatar, Oman, and Bahrain, 2009.

30. In 1992, Ishida estimated that Japanese firms accounted for only 1.1 per cent of overseas firms operating in the Persian Gulf. Ishida. p. 185.

31. Ministry for Foreign Affairs (China), Overview file on the UAE, 2009.

32. Ibid.

33. Bin Huwaidin, *China's Relations with Arabia and the Gulf*, p. 242.

34. *Financial Times*, 18 Jan. 2010.

35. *Arabian Business*, 31 Mar. 2008.

36. Nakheel press release on Dragonmart, Jan. 2009.

37. Calabrese, 'The Consolidation of Gulf-Asia Relations', p. 7.

38. *Gulf Daily News*, 3 Aug. 2009.

39. Davidson, *Dubai*, pp. 45; 69–70.

40. *The National*, 27 Jul. 2009.

41. *The National*, 2 Dec. 2009.

42. Calabrese, 'The Consolidation of Gulf-Asia Relations', p. 7.

43. Personal interviews with ADTA spokespersons, Abu Dhabi, Dec. 2009.

44. *Saudi Gazette*, 22 Nov. 2009.

45. Ministry for Foreign Affairs (China), Overview file on Saudi Arabia, 2009.

46. Bin Huwaidin, *China's Relations with Arabia and the Gulf, 1949–1999*, pp. 233–234.

47. Yetiv and Lu, *China's Relations with Arabia and the Gulf, 1949–1999*, p. 202.

48. Bin Huwaidin, 'China's Relations with Arabia and the Gulf', p. 234.

49. Ministry for Foreign Affairs (China), Overview file on Saudi Arabia, 2009.

50. Ghafour, 'China's Policy in the Persian Gulf', p. 87.

51. Calabrese, 'The Consolidation of Gulf-Asia Relations', p. 3.

52. Calabrese, John. 'China and the Persian Gulf: Energy and Security' in *Middle East Journal*, vol. 52, no. 3, 1998, p. 358.

53. Bin Huwaidin, *China's Relations with Arabia and the Gulf, 1949–1999*, p. 257.

54. Ministry for Foreign Affairs (Japan), Overview files on Kuwait, Qatar, Oman, and Bahrain, 2009.

55. Yetiv and Lu, 'China, Global Energy, and the Middle East', p. 206.

56. Calabrese, 'The Consolidation of Gulf-Asia Relations', p. 2.

57. Ghafour, 'China's Policy in the Persian Gulf', p. 87; *China Daily*, 30 Jan. 2004; *People's Daily*, 12 Feb. 2009; Gulf Cooperation Council Secretariat. 'Economic Relations between GCC Member States and the People's Republic of China', Riyadh: Studies and Research Department, Jun. 2009.

58. *Arab News*, 24 Mar. 2010.

59. *Zawya Dow Jones*, 8 Mar. 2009.

60. See chapter one.

61. Ehteshami, 'The Rise and Convergence of the "Middle" in the World Economy', p. 148.

62. Ibid., p. 151.

63. Ibid.

64. Ministry for Foreign Affairs (South Korea), Overview files on Saudi Arabia, UAE, Kuwait, Qatar, Oman, and Bahrain, 2009.

65. Calabrese, 'The Consolidation of Gulf-Asia Relations', p. 5.

66. Stott, David A. 'South Korea's Global Nuclear Ambitions' in *The Asia-Pacific Journal*, vol. 12, Mar. 2010.

67. Ibid.

68. *Kuwait Times*, 8 Mar. 2009.

5. INVESTMENTS AND JOINT VENTURES

1. *The National*, 2 Nov. 2009.

2. *Arab News*, 7 May 2009. Quoting Nicholas Janardhan.

3. Janardhan, Nicholas, speaking at the 'China in the Arab World and Emerging East Asia-Middle East Nexus' conference, Durham University, 29 Sept. 2009.

4. Ghafour, 'China's Policy in the Persian Gulf', p. 83.

5. Ministry for Finance (Japan), 2009.

6. *Saudi Gazette*, 22 Jul. 2009.

7. Calabrese, 'The Consolidation of Gulf-Asia Relations', p. 3.

8. *Reuters*, 11 Aug. 2009; *Kuwait Times*, 11 Aug. 2009.

9. *Saudi Gazette*, 12 Oct. 2009.

10. Ministry for Foreign Affairs (Japan), Overview file on Saudi Arabia, 2009.

11. Showa Shell Sekiyu press release, 24 Jun. 2009.

12. Ministry for Finance (Japan), 2009.

13. *Associated Press*, 2 Aug. 2009.

14. *Arabian Business*, 26 Nov. 2007.

15. *Reuters*, 4 Nov. 2009.

16. Ministry for Foreign Affairs (Japan), Overview file on the UAE, 2009.

17. Ministry for Foreign Affairs (Japan), Overview files on Qatar and Oman, 2009.

18. Calabrese, 'The Consolidation of Gulf-Asia Relations', p. 5.

19. Ghafour, 'China's Policy in the Persian Gulf', p. 87.

20. Yetiv and Lu, 'China, Global Energy, and the Middle East', p. 205.

21. Ehteshami, 'The Rise and Convergence of the "Middle" in the World Economy', p. 151.

22. Calabrese, 'China and the Persian Gulf: Energy and Security'; Bin Huwaidin, *China's Relations with Arabia and the Gulf*, p. 194.

23. Ibid.

24. Ibid.

25. Calabrese, 'The Consolidation of Gulf-Asia Relations', p. 5.

26. *Washington Post*, 9 Apr. 2007

27. The facilities were originally going to be built at Nansha City, but in 2009 the location was changed to Zhanjiang City.

28. *Associated Press*, 26 Jun. 2009.

29. Ghafour, 'China's Policy in the Persian Gulf', p. 89.

30. See for example, the recent agreements between the UAE and Pakistan. *Gulf News*, 7 Oct. 2009.

31. *Financial Times*, 10 Jul. 2009.

32. Janardhan, 'China in the Arab World and Emerging East Asia-Middle East Nexus'.

33. Lee and Shalmon, 'Searching for Oil: China's Oil Initiatives in the Middle East', pp. 4–5.

34. *Saudi Gazette*, 21 Nov. 2009.

35. Ibid.

36. Yetiv and Lu, 'China, Global Energy, and the Middle East', pp. 207–208.

37. *The National*, 2 Dec. 2009.

38. Ghafour, 'China's Policy in the Persian Gulf', pp. 87–88.

39. Lee and Shalmon, 'Searching for Oil: China's Oil Initiatives in the Middle East', p. 17.

40. Ibid.

41. Calabrese, 'The Consolidation of Gulf-Asia Relations', p. 3.

42. Ghafour, 'China's Policy in the Persian Gulf', p. 87.

43. *Financial Times*, 2 Nov. 2009.

44. *Gulf Times*, 6 Aug. 2009.

45. *Financial Times*, 24 Feb. 2010.

46. *Gulf Times*, 7 Nov. 2009.

47. Ehteshami, 'The Rise and Convergence of the "Middle" in the World Economy', p. 151.

48. Bin Huwaidin, *China's Relations with Arabia and the Gulf*, p. 243.

49. Calabrese, 'The Consolidation of Gulf-Asia Relations', p. 4.

50. *The National*, 21 Jul. 2009.

51. Ibid.

52. Calabrese, 'The Consolidation of Gulf-Asia Relations', p. 2.

53. *AMEInfo*, 14 Apr. 2008.

54. Personal interviews, Dubai International Financial Centre, Dubai, Dec. 2009.

55. See chapter six.

56. *Emirates Business 24*, 14 Oct. 2009.

57. Personal interviews, Dubai International Financial Centre, Dubai, Dec. 2009.

58. *Arabian Business*, 28 Mar. 2010.

59. Calabrese, 'The Consolidation of Gulf-Asia Relations', pp. 4–5.

60. *Financial Times*, 18 Jan. 2010.

61. *Saudi Gazette*, 22 Nov. 2009.

62. Bin Huwaidin, *China's Relations with Arabia and the Gulf*, p. 250. The Abu Dhabi Chamber of Commerce and Industry proposed this project in 1997.

63. Ibid., p. 101; *The National*, 5 Aug. 2008.

64. Calabrese, 'The Consolidation of Gulf-Asia Relations', p. 5.

65. Personal interviews, Abu Dhabi, Dec. 2009.

66. *The National*, 23 Feb. 2010. Quoting Ben Simpfendorfer, the chief China economist at the Royal Bank of Scotland in Hong Kong.

67. Ibid.

68. Mubadala Development Corporation, Press release on Pearl Energy, Jan. 2009.

69. *The National*, 21 Jul. 2009, Mubadala Development Corporation, Press release on Pearl Energy, Jan. 2009.

70. See chapter nine.

71. *Korea Times*, 26 Oct. 2009.

72. Davidson, *Abu Dhabi*, p. 82–83.

73. ATIC press release, 19 Jan. 2010.

74. *Bloomberg*, 18 Jan. 2010.

75. *Gulf Today*, 16 Oct. 2009; Stott, 'South Korea's Global Nuclear Ambitions'.

6. CONSTRUCTION AND LABOUR CONTRACTS

1. Bin Huwaidin, *China's Relations with Arabia and the Gulf*, p. 195.

2. Ehteshami, 'The Rise and Convergence of the "Middle" in the World Economy', p. 148.

3. Calabrese, 'China and the Persian Gulf', p. 357.

4. Bin Huwaidin, *China's Relations with Arabia and the Gulf*, p. 201.

5. Ibid., p. 249.

6. Lee, and Shalmon, 'Searching for Oil: China's Oil Initiatives in the Middle East', p. 15.

7. Bin Huwaidin, *China's Relations with Arabia and the Gulf*, p. 234.

8. For example, a Chinese company supplied the labour for the new Rotana Hotel in Fujairah.

9. Personal interviews, Japanese Ministry for Foreign Affairs, Japan, August 2009.

10. *The National*, 20 Jul. 2009.

11. Calabrese, 'The Consolidation of Gulf-Asia Relations', p. 4.

12. Personal interviews, Paris, Mar. 2010.

13. Janardhan, 'China in the Arab World and Emerging East Asia-Middle East Nexus'.

14. Calabrese, 'The Consolidation of Gulf-Asia Relations', p. 4.

15. *The National*, 24 Mar. 2010.

16. Janardhan, 'China in the Arab World and Emerging East Asia-Middle East Nexus'.

17. *Saudi Gazette*, 26 Jul. 2009.

18. *Associated Press*, 26 Jun. 2009.

19. *Middle East Economic Digest*, 19 Jun. 2009.

20. Ehteshami, 'The Rise and Convergence of the "Middle" in the World Economy', p. 168.

21. Ibid., pp. 148–149.

22. *Middle East Economic Digest*, 19 Jun. 2009.

23. *Korea Times*, 19 Feb. 2010.

24. Ibid.

25. See chapter eight.

26. Personal interviews, Abu Dhabi, Dec. 2009.

27. *Middle East Economic Digest*, 19 Jun. 2009.

28. See chapter nine.

29. *Reuters*, 20 Oct. 2009.

30. *Middle East Economic Digest*, 19 Jun. 2009.

31. Ibid.

32. *Korea Times*, 19 Feb. 2010.

33. *Arabian Business*, 19 Nov. 2009.

34. *Agence France-Presse*, 2 Mar. 2010.

35. *Korea Times*, 19 Feb. 2010.

36. Stott, 'South Korea's Global Nuclear Ambitions'.

37. *Korea Herald*, 17 Jul. 2009.

38. *Khaleej Times*, 12 Oct. 2009.

39. *Middle East Economic Digest*, 19 Jun. 2009.

40. *Arabian Business*, 4 Dec. 2009 Quoting EFG-Hermes.

41. Davidson, *Dubai*, p. 151.

42. Personal interviews, Dubai, Dec. 2009.

43. The non-Japanese company was Turkey's Yapi Merkezi.

44. See for example, *Gulf News*, 10 Sept. 2009.

45. *Financial Times*, 16 Feb. 2010.

46. *The National*, 7 Nov. 2009.

47. In mid-December 2009, the government of Abu Dhabi provided Dubai with an additional bailout package of $10 billion. Most of this package was believed to be intended for the payment of contractors. *Reuters*, 14 Dec. 2009.

48. *The National*, 7 Nov. 2009.

49. *Gulf News*, 13 Nov. 2009.

7. AN ASIAN SECURITY UMBRELLA?

1. The UAE Armed Forces, for example, has several thousand expatriates serving in its ranks, and expatriates likely make up the bulk of the army's lower ranks. Davidson, *Abu Dhabi*, p. 144.

2. See for example, the various chapters in Kostiner, Joseph (ed.). *Middle East Monarchies: The Challenge of Modernity*, Boulder: Lynne Rienner, 2000.

3. Bin Huwaidin, *China's Relations with Arabia and the Gulf*, p. 5.

4. Ibid., p. 208.

5. Ibid., p. 115; Dillon, 'The Middle East and China', p. 48.

6. Bin Huwaidin, *China's Relations with Arabia and the Gulf*, p. 225.

7. Ibid., p. 230.

8. Ibid., p. 225.

9. Ibid., pp. 115–116.

10. Dillion, 'The Middle East and China', p. 48.

11. Lee and Shalmon, 'Searching for Oil: China's Oil Initiatives in the Middle East', pp. 12–13, 18.

12. Calabrese, 'China and the Persian Gulf: Energy and Security', p. 363.

13. Bin Huwaidin, *China's Relations with Arabia and the Gulf*, p. 193.

14. Calabrese, China and the Persian Gulf: Energy and Security', p. 363.

15. Bin Huwaidin, *China's Relations with Arabia and the Gulf*, p. 200.

16. Ibid., p. 232.

17. Ibid., p. 255; 260.

18. *Disarmament Diplomacy*, 14 Apr. 1997.

19. Ehteshami, 'The Rise and Convergence of the "Middle" in the World Economy', p. 12.

20. Nuclear Threat Initiative. *China's Missile Exports and Assistance to the Middle East*, Monterey: James Martin Center for Non-proliferation Studies, 2007.

21. *New York Times*, 31 Jan. 2010; *Washington Post*, 30 Jan. 2010.

22. This $7 billion purchase was agreed in 1998. *Washington Post*, 13 May 1998.

23. *Washington Post*, 30 Jan. 2010.

24. Personal interviews, Abu Dhabi, Dec. 2009.

25. *Washington Post*, 27 May 2009.

26. *New York Times*, 31 Jan. 2010.

27. Yetiv, and Lu, 'China, Global Energy, and the Middle East', pp. 200–201.

28. Article 9 of the Japanese constitution states: 'aspiring sincerely to an international peace based on justice and order, the Japanese people forever renounce war as a sovereign right of the nation and the threat or use of force as means of settling international disputes. To accomplish the aim of the preceding paragraph, land, sea, and air forces, as well as other war potential, will never be maintained. The right of belligerency of the state will not be recognized.'

29. Ishida, 'Japan's Oil Strategy in the Gulf without Arms Deals', p. 190.

30. Dillion, 'The Middle East and China', p. 48.

31. Bin Huwaidin, *China's Relations with Arabia and the Gulf*, pp. 102–103.

32. Ibid.

33. Calabrese, John. 'From Flyswatters to Silkworms: The Evolution of China's Role in West Asia' in *Asian Survey*, vol. 30, 1990. p. 867; Ghafour, 'China's Policy in the Persian Gulf', pp. 89; 91.

34. Dillion, 'The Middle East and China', p. 49.

35. Lin, Christina. 'China's Persian Gulf Strategy: Israel and a Nuclearizing Iran' in *China Brief*, vol. 9, no. 21, 2009.

36. Bin Huwaidin, *China's Relations with Arabia and the Gulf*, p. 116.

37. A notable exception being the emirate of Dubai, which has long considered Iran to be a principal trading partner. See Dillon, 'The Middle East and China' p. 49; Davidson, *Dubai*, pp. 71–76.

38. *Beijing Review*, no. 39, 29 Sept. 1980. p. 5.

39. Bin Huwaidin, *China's Relations with Arabia and the Gulf*, p. 195.

40. Ibid., p. 113.; Lin, 'China's Persian Gulf Strategy'.

41. Bin Huwaidin, *China's Relations with Arabia and the Gulf*, p. 243.

42. Dillion, 'The Middle East and China', p. 52.

43. Bin Huwaidin, *China's Relations with Arabia and the Gulf*, pp. 116–117.

44. Ibid., p. 120.

45. Ibid., p. 121.

46. Ibid., p. 122.

47. Calabrese, 'China and the Persian Gulf', p. 360.

48. Bin Huwaidin, *China's Relations with Arabia and the Gulf*, p. 121.

49. Rubin, Barry, 'China's Middle East Strategy' in *China Report*, vol. 34, 1998, p. 352.

50. Lee and Shalmon, p. 23.

51. Dillion, 'The Middle East and China', p. 50.

52. Ghafour, pp. 88–89, 91; Yetiv and Lu, p. 211.

53. Bin Huwaidin, *China's Relations with Arabia and the Gulf*, p. 200.

54. Ghafour, pp. 88–89, 91; Yetiv and Lu, p. 211.

55. Rubin, 'China's Middle East Strategy', p. 352.

56. Calabrese, 'China and the Persian Gulf', pp. 360–361.

57. Rubin, 'China's Middle East Strategy', p. 352.

58. Ehteshami 1991, p. 12; Dillion, 'The Middle East and China', p. 47.

59. Ibid., p. 48.

60. Ministry for Foreign Affairs (China), Overview file on Kuwait, 2009.

61. *Times of India*, 13 Sept. 2009.

62. *The National*, 24 Mar. 2010.

63. Janardhan, 'China in the Arab World and Emerging East Asia-Middle East Nexus'.

64. *People's Daily*, 15 Aug. 2009.

65. Personal interviews, Japanese Ministry for Foreign Affairs, Japan, Aug. 2009.

66. *The National*, 23 Mar. 2010.

67. *South China Morning Post*, 27 Mar. 2010.

68. *The National*, 24 Mar. 2010.

69. See chapter nine.

70. *United Press International*, 30 Dec. 2009.

71. Calabrese, 'The Consolidation of Gulf-Asia Relations', p. 8.

72. *United Press International*, 30 Dec. 2009.

73. *Financial Times*, 22 Mar. 2010.

74. See chapter nine.

75. *United Press International*, 17 Feb. 2010.

76. Calabrese, 'The Consolidation of Gulf-Asia Relations', pp. 8–9.

8. DIPLOMACY AND DIALOGUE

1. Personal interviews, Japanese Ministry for Foreign Affairs, Aug. 2009.

2. Calabrese, 'The Consolidation of Gulf-Asia Relations', p. 2.

3. See chapter one.

4. Personal interviews, Japanese Ministry for Foreign Affairs, Aug. 2009.

5. Ishida, 'Japan's Oil Strategy in the Gulf without Arms Deals', p. 187.

6. Ibid., p. 187.

7. Stott, 'Japan and the United Arab Emirates', p. 7.

8. Personal interviews, Japanese Ministry for Foreign Affairs, Aug. 2009.

9. Ishida, 'Japan's Oil Strategy in the Gulf without Arms Deals', p. 189.

10. Personal interviews, Japanese Ministry for Foreign Affairs, Aug. 2009.

11. *Khaleej Times*, 11 Oct. 2009.

12. Stott, 'Japan and the United Arab Emirates', p. 7.

13. Ministry for Foreign Affairs (Japan), Overview files on Saudi Arabia and the UAE, 2009.

14. Ministry for Foreign Affairs (Japan), Overview file on Qatar, 2009.

15. *Associated Press*, 26 May 2009.

16. *Gulf Times*, 17 Nov. 2009.

17. About $103,500 in 2009. See chapter two.

18. *Gulf Times*, 12 Oct. 2009.

19. Ministry for Foreign Affairs (Japan), Overview files on Oman and Bahrain, 2009.

20. See chapter one.

21. See for example, Yetiv and Lu's discussion of Saudi Arabia's repression of its Shia minorities and its similarities with Chinese repression of Muslim communities. Yetiv and Lu, 'China, Global Energy, and the Middle East', p. 202.

22. Bin Huwaidin, *China's Relations with Arabia and the Gulf*, p. 255.

23. Personal interviews, Japanese Ministry for Foreign Affairs, Aug. 2009.

24. Dillon, 'The Middle East and China', p. 42.

25. Niblock, 'China in the Arab World and Emerging East Asia-Middle East Nexus'.

26. Bin Huwaidin, *China's Relations with Arabia and the Gulf*, p. 214.

27. Dillon, 'The Middle East and China', p. 48.

28. Bin Huwaidin, *China's Relations with Arabia and the Gulf*, p. 214

29. Ibid., p. 230. Quoting the Saudi government subsidised newspaper *Al-Riyadh*.

30. Ibid., p. 239. Quoting the UAE government newspaper *Al-Wahdah*.

31. Ibid., p. 257.

32. *The National*, 15 Aug. 2009.

33. *Arab News*, 24 Mar. 2010.

34. Personal interviews, Japanese Ministry for Foreign Affairs, Aug. 2009.

35. Niblock, 'China in the Arab World and Emerging East Asia-Middle East Nexus'.

36. *New Yorker*, 15 Jun. 2009. Quoting Ben Simpfendorfer.

37. See chapter four.

38. *The National*, 1 Aug. 2009.

39. Ministry for Foreign Affairs (China), Overview file on Saudi Arabia, 2009.

40. Ghafour, 'China's Policy in the Persian Gulf', pp. 87–88; Bin Huwaidin, *China's Relations with Arabia and the Gulf*, p. 231.

41. Calabrese, 'The Consolidation of Gulf-Asia Relations', p. 2.

42. *Washington Post*, 9 Apr. 2007.

43. Personal interviews, London, Mar. 2010.

44. Bin Huwaidin, *China's Relations with Arabia and the Gulf*, pp. 216–217.

45. Ibid., p. 229.

46. Ministry for Foreign Affairs (China), Overview file on Saudi Arabia, 2009.

47. Ghafour, 'China's Policy in the Persian Gulf', pp. 87–88.

48. Yetiv and Lu, 'China, Global Energy, and the Middle East', p. 205.

49. Bin Huwaidin, *China's Relations with Arabia and the Gulf*, p. 244.

50. Ibid., p. 248.

51. Ibid., p. 246; Personal interviews, London, Mar. 2010.

52. Bin Huwaidin, *China's Relations with Arabia and the Gulf*, p. 248.

53. Ministry for Foreign Affairs (China), Overview file on the UAE, 2009.

54. *Arabian Business*, 31 Mar. 2008.

55. *Kuwait News Agency*, 8 Aug. 2009.

56. *Emirates News Agency (WAM)*, 10 Dec. 2009.

57. Ministry for Foreign Affairs (China), Overview file on the UAE, 2009.

58. Zayed University press release 'Destined to Lead,' Oct. 2009.

59. Bin Huwaidin, *China's Relations with Arabia and the Gulf*, p. 196. Quoting the *Kuwait Times*.

60. Ministry for Foreign Affairs (China), Overview file on Kuwait, 2009.

61. Bin Huwaidin, *China's Relations with Arabia and the Gulf*, p. 198.

62. Ibid., p. 194.

63. Ibid., pp. 200–201.

64. Ghafour, 'China's Policy in the Persian Gulf', pp. 87; 89; Ministry for Foreign Affairs (China), Overview file on Kuwait, 2009.

65. Bin Huwaidin, *China's Relations with Arabia and the Gulf*, p. 199.

66. Ministry for Foreign Affairs (China), Overview file on Qatar,2009; Bin Huwaidin, *China's Relations with Arabia and the Gulf*, p. 254.

67. *Gulf News*, 14 Nov. 2009.

68. Bin Huwaidin, *China's Relations with Arabia and the Gulf*, p. 208.

69. See chapter one.

70. Bin Huwaidin, *China's Relations with Arabia and the Gulf*, p. 209.

71. Ministry for Foreign Affairs (China), Overview files on Qatar and Oman, 2009.

72. Ministry for Foreign Affairs (China), Overview file on Bahrain, 2009.

73. Personal interviews, Japanese Ministry for Foreign Affairs, Aug. 2009.

74. *Washington Post*, 9 Apr. 2007.

75. Ministry for Foreign Affairs (South Korea), Overview file on the UAE, 2009.

76. ATIC press release, 19 Jan. 2010.

77. *The National*, 23 Feb. 2010.

78. *AMEInfo*, 14 Jan. 2010.

79. Ministry for Foreign Affairs (South Korea), Overview files on Saudi Arabia, the UAE, Kuwait, and Qatar, 2009.

80. *Associated Press*, 25 Jun. 2009.

81. *Gulf Times*, 7 Nov. 2009.

82. Ministry for Foreign Affairs (South Korea), Overview file on Oman and Bahrain, 2009.

9. FUTURE INITIATIVES AND COLLABORATIONS

1. For a discussion of potential energy rivalries between the United States and China see for example, Moran, Daniel, and Russell, James (eds), *Energy Security and Global Politics: The Militarization of Resource Management*, London: Routledge, 2008.

2. See chapter one.

3. Lee, and Shalmon, 'Searching for Oil: China's Oil Initiatives in the Middle East', p. 18.

4. Personal interviews, London, Mar. 2010.

5. *APS Review*, 'Oil Market Trends' 14 Dec. 2009.

6. *Financial Times*, 21 Feb. 2010; *Oil and Gas Journal*, 12 Jan. 2010.

7. *Reuters*, 20 Mar. 2009.

8. *The National*, 26 Jun. 2009.

9. Calabrese, 'The Consolidation of Gulf-Asia Relations'. p. 8.

10. For a discussion of Masdar City, see Davidson, *Abu Dhabi*, pp. 84–85.

11. Personal interviews, Japanese Ministry for Foreign Affairs, Japan, Aug. 2009.

12. *Associated Press*, 25 Jun. 2009.

13. *Bloomberg*, 24 Jan. 2010.

14. *Kyodo News*, 19 Oct. 2009.

15. *Associated Press*, 19 Nov. 2009.

16. *The National*, 28 Dec. 2009.

17. *Arirang*, 3 Mar. 2010.

18. Niblock, 'China in the Arab World and Emerging East Asia-Middle East Nexus'.

19. *The National*, 6 Aug. 2009.

20. Calabrese, 'The Consolidation of Gulf-Asia Relations', p. 4.

21. Ghafour, 'China's Policy in the Persian Gulf', p. 83.

22. *Financial Times*, 2 Mar. 2010.

23. Bin Huwaidin, *China's Relations with Arabia and the Gulf*, p. 233.

24. Ibid., Quoting the BBC and the *New York Times*.

25. Stott, 'Japan and the United Arab Emirates', p. 8.

26. Ibid., p. 5.

27. Ibid., p. 5.

28. Ibid., p. 6.

29. Ibid., p. 6.

30. *The National*, 27 Dec. 2009.

31. *AMEInfo*, 25 Feb. 2010.

32. The video was broadcast on 22 Apr. 2009 by ABC News.

33. The video has been circulating on www.uaetorture.com since summer 2008.

34. *Vanity Fair*, 22 Jul. 2009.

35. Ibid.

36. Personal interviews, London, Sept. 2009.

37. *The National*, 28 Oct. 2009.

38. See www.usuaebusiness.org for a full list of founding members.

39. ENEC press release, 27 Dec. 2009.

40. Stott, 'Japan and the United Arab Emirates', pp. 4–5.

41. *Middle East Economic Digest*, 8 Jan. 2010.

42. *Korea Teams*, 12 Jan. 2010.

43. *Middle East Economic Digest*, 8 Jan. 2010; Stott, David A., 'South Korea's Global Nuclear Ambitions' in *The Asia-Pacific Journal*, vol. 12, Mar. 2010.

44. *Power-Gen Worldwide*, 3 Mar. 2010.

45. *Business Week*, 2 Mar. 2010.

46. *Asia Pulse*, 3 Aug. 2009; *Platts*, 11 Aug. 2009.

47. *Utilities-ME*, 19 Nov. 2009.

48. *The National*, 28 Dec. 2009; Stott, 'South Korea's Global Nuclear Ambitions'.

49. *Korea Herald*, 9 Feb. 2010.

50. *Korea Times*, 12 Jan. 2010.

51. *The National*, 28 Dec. 2009.

52. *Middle East Economic Digest*, 8 Jan. 2010.

53. *Yonhap News*, 2 Feb. 2010.

54. *Arirang*, 18 Feb. 2010; *The National*, 21 Mar 2010; Stott, 'South Korea's Global Nuclear Ambitions'.

55. Stott, 'Japan and the United Arab Emirates', p. 6.

56. *Arirang*, 16 Feb. 2010.

BIBLIOGRAPHY

Abidi, A., *China, Iran, and the Persian Gulf,* New Delhi: Radiant, 1982.

Adie, W., 'China's Middle East Strategy' in *The World Today*, vol. 23, 1967.

Al-Alkim, H., *The Foreign Policy of the United Arab Emirates*, London: Saqi, 1988.

Ayubi, Nazih N., 'OPEC and the Third World: The Case of Arab Aid' in Stookey, Robert W (ed.), *The Arabian Peninsula: Zone of Ferment*, Stanford: Hoover Institution Press, 1984.

Azar, E., 'Soviet and Chinese Roles in the Middle East' in *Problems of Communism*, vol. 28, no. 3, 1979

Baum, R. (ed.), *China's Four Modernizations: The New Technological Revolution*, Boulder: Westview, 1980.

Behbehani, H., *China's Foreign Policy in the Arab World, 1955–1975*, London: KPI, 1981.

Behbehani, H. (ed.), *China and the People's Democratic Republic of Yemen*, London: KPI, 1985.

Buxani, Ram, *Taking the High Road*, Dubai: Motivate, 2003.

Calabrese, John, 'From Flyswatters to Silkworms: The Evolution of China's Role in West Asia' in *Asian Survey*, vol. 30, 1990.

Calabrese, John, *China's changing relations with the Middle East*, New York: Pinter, 1991.

Calabrese, John, 'China and the Persian Gulf: Energy and Security' in *Middle East Journal*, vol. 52, no. 3, 1998.

Calabrese, John, 'The Consolidation of Gulf-Asia Relations: Washington Tuned in or Out of Touch?' policy brief published by the Middle East Institute, Washington DC, Jun. 2009.

Cheung, T., 'Unguided Missiles: China's Arms Exports Stir Consternation' in *Far Eastern Economic Review*, Feb. 1992.

Chou, S., 'China's Foreign Trade Relations' in *Current History*, vol. 83, Sept. 1984.

Davidson, Christopher M., *The United Arab Emirates: A Study in Survival*, Boulder: Lynne Rienner Press, 2005.

Davidson, Christopher M., *Dubai: The Vulnerability of Success*, New York: Columbia University Press, 2008.

Davidson, Christopher M., *Abu Dhabi: Oil and Beyond*, New York: Columbia University Press, 2009.

Davies, Charles E. (ed.), *Global Interests in the Arab Gulf*, Exeter: University of Exeter Press, 1992.

Delfs, R., 'The Gulf Card' in *Far Eastern Economic Review*, vol. 149, Sept. 1990.

Denoon, D. and Frieman, W., 'China's Security Strategy: The View from Beijing, Asia, and Washington' in *Asian Survey*, vol. 36, no. 4, 1996.

Dibb, P., 'The Revolution in Military Affairs and Asian Security' in *Survival*, vol. 39, no. 4, 1997.

Dillon, Michael, 'The Middle East and China' in Ehteshami, Anoushivaran, and Carter, Hannah (eds). *The Middle East's Relations with Asia and Russia*, London: Routledge, 2004.

Disney, N., *China and the Middle East*, Washington DC: MERIP, 1977.

Ehteshami, Anoushivaran, 'The Rise and Convergence of the "Middle" in the World Economy: The Case of the NICs and the Gulf States' in Davies, Charles E. (ed.), *Global Interests in the Arab Gulf*, Exeter: University of Exeter Press, 1992.

Ehteshami, Anoushivaran (ed.), *From the Gulf to Central Asia: Players in the New Great Game*, Exeter: University of Exeter Press, 1994.

Ehteshami, Anoushivaran, 'The Changing Balance of Power in Asia' in *ECSSR Occasional Papers*, 1998.

Ehteshami, Anoushivaran, and Carter, Hannah (eds), *The Middle East's Relations with Asia and Russia*, London: Routledge, 2004.

Ehteshami, Anoushivaran, 'Asian Geostrategic Realities and their Impact on Middle East-Asia Relations' in Ehteshami, Anoushivaran, and Carter, Hannah (eds), *The Middle East's Relations with Asia and Russia*, London: Routledge, 2004.

Evans, Richard, *Deng Xiaoping and the Making of Modern China*, London: Penguin, 1995.

Faust, J., *China in World Politics*, Boulder: Lynne Rienner Press, 1995.

Freeze, R., 'The Arab and China' in *Arab Report*, no. 3, Feb. 1979.

Funabashi, Yoichi, 'The Asianization of Asia' in *Foreign Affairs*, Dec. 1993.

Ghafour, Mahmoud, 'China's Policy in the Persian Gulf' in *Middle East Policy*, vol. 16, no. 2, 2009.

Glaser, B., 'China's Security Perceptions, Interests, and Ambitions' in *Asian Survey*, vol. 32, no. 3, 1993.

Halliday, F., *Revolution and Foreign Policy: The Case of South Yemen, 1967–1987*, Cambridge: Cambridge University Press, 1990.

Harding, H., *China's Foreign Relations in the 1980s*, New Haven: Yale University Press, 1984.

Harris, L., *China Considers the Middle East*, New York: IB Tauris, 1993.

Bin Huwaidin, Muhammed, *China's Relations with Arabia and the Gulf, 1949–1999*, London: Routledge, 2002.

Bin Huwaidin, Muhammed, 'Determinants of Saudi Arabia's Foreign Policy Towards China' in *Journal of Strategic Studies*, vol. 3, no. 7, 2007.

Hsu, I., *The Rise of Modern China*, Oxford: Oxford University Press, 1990.

Huo, H., 'Patterns of Behaviour in China's Foreign Policy, the Gulf Crisis, and Beyond' in *Asian Survey*, vol. 32, Mar. 1992.

Ishida, Susumu, 'Japan's Oil Strategy in the Gulf without Arms Deals' in Davies, Charles E. (ed.), *Global Interests in the Arab Gulf*, Exeter: University of Exeter Press, 1992.

Kechichian, J., *Oman and the World: The Emergence of an Independent Foreign Policy*, Santa Monica: Rand, 1995.

Kemp, G., 'The Persian Gulf Remains the Strategic Prize' in *Survival*, vol. 40, no. 4, 1998.

Kim, S. (ed.), *China and the World: Chinese Foreign Relations in the Post-Cold War Era*, Boulder: Westview, 1994.

Kostiner, Joseph (ed.), *Middle East Monarchies: The Challenge of Modernity*, Boulder: Lynne Rienner, 2000.

Kumaraswamy, P.R. (ed.), *China and the Middle East: The Quest for Influence*, New Delhi and London: Sage, 1999.

Kumaraswamy, P.R., 'China and Israel: Normalization and After' in Kumaraswamy, P.R. (ed.), *China and the Middle East: The Quest for Influence*, New Delhi and London: Sage, 1999.

Lawrence, A., *China's Foreign Relations Since 1949*, London: Routledge, 1975.

Lee, Henry, and Shalmon, Dan, 'Searching for Oil: China's Oil Initiatives in the Middle East' discussion paper published by the Environment and Natural Resources Program, Belfer Center for Science and International Affairs Discussion Paper, Harvard University, Jan. 2007.

Legum, C. (ed.), *Crisis and Conflicts in the Middle East: The Changing Strategy*, New York: Holmes, 1981.

Lin, Christina, 'China's Persian Gulf Strategy: Israel and a Nuclearizing Iran' in *China Brief*, vol. 9, no. 21, 2009.

Miyagi, Yukiko, *Japan's Middle East Security Policy*, Routledge: London, 2008.

Moran, Daniel, and Russell, James (eds), *Energy Security and Global Politics: The Militarization of Resource Management*, London: Routledge, 2008.

Mosher, S., *Hegemon: China's Plan to Dominate Asia and the World*, San Francisco: Encounter, 2000.

Onley, James, *The Arabian Frontier of the British Raj: Merchants, Rulers, and the British in the Nineteenth-Century Gulf*, Oxford: Oxford University Press, 2007.

Parker, M., 'Saudi-China: Chinese Trade Takes Off' in *The Middle East*, Oct. 1993.

Quandt, W., *Saudi Arabia in the 1980s: Foreign Policy, Security, and Oil*, Washington DC: Brookings, 1981.

Robinson, T., 'Interdependence in China's Foreign Relations' in Kim, S. (ed.), *China and the World: Chinese Foreign Relations in the Post-Cold War Era*, Boulder: Westview, 1994.

Rubin, Barry, 'China's Middle East Strategy' in *China Report*, vol. 34, 1998.

Rubin, Barry, 'China's Middle East Strategy' in Kumaraswamy, P.R. (ed.), *China and the Middle East: The Quest for Influence*, New Delhi and London: Sage, 1999.

Safran, N., *Saudi Arabia: The Ceaseless Quest for Security*, New York: Cornell University Press, 1988.

Saxonhouse, Gary, and Stern, Robert (eds), *Japan's Lost Decade: Origins, Consequences and Prospects for Recovery*, London: Wiley, 2004.

Shichor, Y., *The Middle East in China's Foreign Policy, 1949–1977*, Cambridge: Cambridge University Press, 1979.

Shichor, Y., 'The Role of Islam in China's Middle Eastern Policy' in Israel, R., and John, A. (eds), *Islam in Asia: Southeast and East Asia*, Jerusalem: Magnes, 1984.

Shichor, Y., 'Unfolded Arms: Beijing's Recent Military Sales Offensive' in *Pacific Review*, vol. 1, no. 3, 1988.

Shichor, Y., *East Wind Over Arabia: Origins and Implications of the Sino-Saudi Missile Deal*, Berkeley: University of California Press, 1989.

Shichor, Y., 'China and the Gulf Crisis: Escape from Predicament' in *Problems of Communism*, no. 40, Nov. 1991.

Shichor, Y., 'China and the Role of the United Nations in the Middle East: Revised Policy' in *Asian Survey*, no. 31, Mar. 1991.

Simpfendorfer, Ben, *The New Silk Road: How a Rising Arab World is Turning Away from the West and Rediscovering China*, London: Palgrave, 2009.

Stookey, Robert W. (ed.), *The Arabian Peninsula: Zone of Ferment*, Stanford: Hoover Institution Press, 1984.

Stott, David A., 'Japan and the United Arab Emirates: A Nuclear Family?' in *The Asia-Pacific Journal*, vol. 33, Aug. 2009.

Stott, David A., 'South Korea's Global Nuclear Ambitions' in *The Asia-Pacific Journal*, vol. 12, Mar. 2010.

Tanzer, A., 'The Saudi Connection' in *Far Eastern Economic Review*, Jul. 1982.

Vivoda, Vlado, 'Diversification of Oil Import Sources and Energy Security: A Key Strategy or an Elusive Objective?' in *Energy Policy*, vol. 37, no. 11, 2009.

Wang, T., 'Competition for Friendship: The Two Chinas and Saudi Arabia' in *Arab Studies Quarterly*, vol. 15, no. 3, 1993.

Westad, O. (ed.), *Brothers in Arms: The Rise and Fall of the Sino-Soviet Alliance, 1945–1963*, Stanford: Stanford University Press, 1998.

Wingrove, P. (ed.), *China in the 1990s*, London: Macmillan, 1995.

Yahuda, M., 'Dilemmas and Problems for China in the Middle East' in Legum, C (ed.), *Crisis and Conflicts in the Middle East: The Changing Strategy*, New York: Holmes, 1981.

Yetiv, Steve A. and Lu, Chunlong, 'China, Global Energy, and the Middle East' in *Middle East Journal*, vol. 61, no. 2, 2007.

INDEX